Author: Phillip Ray Garriss
Illustrators: Phillip and Christy Garriss

Date: 2019

Acknowledgements

I am thankful for my family, Corning, PPD, Global River Church, and ATS.

Common Core Computer Programming

General And Advanced Distributed System Programming

Overview:

With over seventeen years of experience in the computer programming field, the author provides techniques, examples, and references that the reader can use to provide high quality and effective business related software solutions. The book is riddled with Tips and advanced programming techniques for many of the popular programming environments. This book will give readers a well spring of knowledge within this field.

The book includes references and examples for HTML, Java, Oracle, .NET, MS Access, and VBA, as well as some other languages and computer tools. Most of these concepts were gleaned from school, books, websites, and on the job experience. Some techniques were developed by the author. Keep in mind that most languages attempt to provide similar programming functionality. Even if the reader is not able to find exactly what he or she is looking for, the book will provide similar scenarios and references to serve as guide lines for most any programming project at hand.

It is assumed that the reader has knowledge of basic programming techniques. He or he should be familiar with common computer concepts like Operating Systems and If and Or Statements before reading this book.

Inline references will provide the links or the books where the original ideas were researched or discovered. In some cases, the general technique from the source remains, but the code has been modified. Tips and Examples are used throughout the book to clarify what is being discussed. There are also Internet references to Walkthroughs where readers can gain additional knowledge by implementing programming examples.

This is an ideal reference tool. In many cases it provides a level of guidance for developers who have limited on the job Internet access. It provides a gold mine of information gained while acquiring programming related certifications, teaching computer classes at Miller Motte, and completing a Masters of Science In Computers Science and Information Systems at UNCW.

Table Of Contents

TOC Note: To build a TOC in MS Word, select a header and choose a Style, or click Alt+Shift+o to create a TC tag. Then go to Insert, Reference, Index and Tables, Table of Contents, Options, select Entry Fields. Click OK.

.NET

In this chapter:

1. An Introduction to Visual Studio .NET
2. .NET Languages
3. Common Commands
4. The Global Assembly Cache and Additional Framework Information
5. .NET Errors
6. Additional .NET topics

An Introduction to Visual Studio .NET

This Microsoft Integrated Development Environment (IDE) allows developers to create software using different languages such as ASP, C#, Java, and VB, as well as several additional supportive languages. It integrates well with the Microsoft Operating System, has a friendly support system for the developer (offering intelliSense typing and coding examples) and can be used to develop a host of application types. Some examples include Console Apps, Internet Forms, and Web Parts for the SharePoint Portal.

The IDE has a menu that is similar to a Word Processor. From the File Menu users can create and save new projects and applications as well as open items that have recently been touched. The Project Menu allows the developer to assign properties for the project, and add directories and references. The build menu allows him or her to debug or run the application. The Help Menu - help about option shows information about the product like its Version and Version Date. The Help Menu - Search allows the developer to search for development topics such as creating combo boxes and list boxes.

Various windows allow the user to edit individual items, such as a C# file using several different views. There is a layout window allowing the user to see what the final product will look like upon completion and a code-behind window for program changes. The code-behind window allows the user to adjust the code that will direct the control items how to perform their tasks. There are many sub windows too, like the control property box that allows the developer to get a closer look at individual .NET items.

Developers can use the setup properties section in the web.config file to automate the application installation process. If certain libraries or application files are needed on the client machine the developer may wish to create a setup file to install these pieces. See the Create A Setup File case study below for information on how to accomplish this.

.NET Languages

.NET allows users to program in a variety of languages. Please note that http://www.tutorialspoint.com/ offers many useful examples and walkthroughs describing how to use these languages. Here is a look at some of the languages Visual Studio .NET provides:

ASP.NET

ASP.NET stands for Active Server Pages. Many websites like the Amazon search page will have an .aspx extension letting people know that it is an active server page. ASP.NET pages can be created without the use of .NET using other editing tools such as Notepad. These pages utilize HTML on the front end to present the data. They use a language of preference on the back end to pull information, manipulate it, and display it in an object such as a list or a data grid. The file used on the back end is referred to as the code behind. The code behind will have trigger references to the frontend HTML objects. For instance, if a developer wants to repopulate a list as it changes, he or she may call the On List change trigger which in turn will use C# with possibly a LINQ to query to pull the data from an ADO connection. If coded correctly, with a professional IDE such as Visual Studio .NET, all of this can be done in a secure, interactive, and professional manner.

C#

C# is another powerful language that works closely with many Operating Systems and their associated Database(s). C# was built using C and C++ as its predecessors. It offers many functions and techniques for pulling data, organizing it in easy to use structures, manipulating it, and presenting it to the customer.

Tip:

Delegates and interfaces are hard concepts in C#. They both interact with a class, but are used at different times. For instance, an interface is used when a class needs to implement one and only one method implementation and a delegate is used when more than one implementation is needed. Take a look at http://msdn.microsoft.com/en-us/library/ms173173(v=vs.90).aspx for additional information.

Java

C, and C+, and C++ are the predecessors to Java. Java incorporates many of the features and functions used in C, but it does it in a more ObjectOriented way.

Tip:

Java is a powerful modern Object Oriented programming language. Read through some of the various Java for Dummies books and the Java chapter in this book to learn more about this exciting subject.

LINQ

Language Integrated Query is a tool used with C#, Java, or VB to select data from an ActiveX Data Object connection. See the Case Study below regarding the setup of a List Box for additional information on how to use LINQ.

TSQL

TSQL or Transact SQL is like Microsoft's version of Oracle PL-SQL. It allows developers to use SQL code within the .NET IDE. Take a look at the T-SQL section in the Database chapter below for additional information.

Visual Basic

Visual Basic is a great programming language for those who want to use visual prompts and illustrations to walk the users through a sophisticated form or wizard. Visual Basic Scripting is closely related to VB and it has been used extensively in the development of various Microsoft Operating Systems.

There are some properties and settings that can be used regardless of the programming language. For example, an XML .config file can be setup to store user information, application key values, and general information about the program. Developers can insert a Web Part control section in the web.config file to establish ground rules for the Web Part behavior, identification, and namespace assignment.

The following is a sample web.config file including a Web Part Control and an application key value.

```
<?xml version="1.0" encoding="utf-8" ?>
<configuration>
<system.web>
<appSettings>
...
<trust level="Full" originUrl="" />
<SafeControls>
<SafeControl
   Assembly="ExampleWebPControl" Version=1.0.0.0,
Culture=neutral, PublicKeyToken=null
   NameSpace="ExampleWebPControl"
   TypeName="*" Safe="True" AllowRemoteDesigner="True" />
</SafeControls>
...
<add key="CustomAppVariable" value="App Text Value"/>
...
</appSettings>
</system.web>
</configuration>
```

Here are a few helpful URLs and notes regarding Web Part controls:

1. http://www.codeproject.com/Articles/25019/Developing-SharePoint-WebParts
2. http://stackoverflow.com/questions/1189364/reading-settings-from-app-config-or-web-config-in-net
3. Note that developer use the System.Configuration ConfigurationManager.AppSettings["CustomAppVariable"] statement to reference information from the setting above.

Common Commands

Some commands, objects, and creation wizards can be run and or utilized regardless of what language the developer chooses to program in. Many of these are very useful for making references and cleaning and removing resource references.

<u>Combo Box</u>

A Combo Box will limit or filter the record selection as the users type. For instance if the Record Group contains hamster, hoot, and horse, and the user types "ho" only hoot and horse will appear as selectable items. Let's give a hoot for Visual Studio .NET! It has a lot to offer.

<u>List Box</u>

A List Box lists all the items in a Record Group. The user must select the item he or she desires as opposed to filtering the records down as he or she is typing.

<u>Global Variables</u>

Global Variables are setup in the web.config file. They are modifiable and can be set at run time or at some other point as a piece of code is being run. Global Variables are not related to Global Warming so they will probably not be mentioned in the next presidential debate. ☺

<u>Start</u>

The Start command can be used to run a program. For instance the

System.Diagnostics.Process.Start('http.google.com'); command will bring up the google website. See http://blogs.msdn.com/b/csharpfaq/archive/2004/06/01/146375.aspx for some additional information on what this command does.

Smart Tags

Smart tags can be created using a class. They will supply a menu interface to the user at run time when he or she clicks on certain items within the application. Take a look at http://msdn.microsoft.com/en-us/library/ms171829.aspx for additional information on smart tags.

Try Catch, and Finally

In any Visual Studio .NET language users can use the Try Catch to look for an error that occurs and throw them as a message to the user or as an error that bounces back to the calling object. Finally is used to clean up objects in memory or possibly as a place to provide the user with a final salutation or message before the code finishes processing. Finally! is also a phrase that is used often in the programming world when our code actually works. ☺

Using

If developers incorporate the Using command followed by a collection of objects the code below that section will have an easier time referencing the associated objects and it will automatically clean up any memory resources used after the code completes. For example, a developer can use the Using System.IO.TextReader command to define a variable that will open a text file, and read it using the TextReader library. He or she might also incorporate the Using command before the form namespace so that items within a library can be easily referenced within the individual procedures and functions. Take a look at Case Study 3 below and http://msdn.microsoft.com/en-us/library/htd05whh.aspx for additional information and examples.

Please note that the author has been using a lot of resources and a lot of caffeine to write this book!

The Global Assembly Cache and Additional Framework Information

GAC stands for Global Assembly Cache. This is where libraries and dlls (dynamic link libraries) are added to a .NET project to allow for additional functionality. References are added from the References – Add – Add Reference menu option. These references are used for any number of things from basic input output with files to creating Web Services with Windows Communication Foundation.

.NET Framework 1.0 was the initial framework used for developing in the .NET IDE. Each supplemental framework provides additional tools and libraries and or adds functionality to those tools. When a .NET project gets created the developer must choose what framework it will run with. Users may also need to download and register the applicable framework on their client computer in order for the various applications to be fully functional.

Tip:

Different frameworks are used for developing richer and fuller technology sets. For example, the Web Part code mentioned a few pages back works with the ASP.NET WebPart Framework available with MOSS 2007. MOSS stands for the Microsoft Office SharePoint Server.

The following case studies will either give the reader a step by step overview or a few external references for how to perform some of the most desired .NET capabilities.

Case Studies

Case Study 1

Web Services:

Web Services can be used to provide a simple value like the date and time, or they can be used to pass an entire database in XML format to an application. The walkthrough found at http://msdn.microsoft.com/en-us/library/bb386386.asp provides a basic understanding of how a web service works. http://msdn.microsoft.com/en-us/library/8wbhsy70(v=vs.80).aspx and http://docs.aws.amazon.com/AWSSdkDocsNET/latest/DeveloperGuide/net-dg-setup.html includes other good Web Service examples.

Tip:

Read Programming Amazon Web Services for additional information.

Tip:

When a developer creates Web Services, he or she should watch out for network routing related issues. For instance, if a message says something like the Barracuda or the X router blocked the request, the developer may need to reach out to the network administrator to find out if a related server or service is being blocked.

Case Study 2

Membership Services:

To develop an application with users and roles a developer can performs steps similar to the ones at these websites:

http://msdn.microsoft.com/en-us/library/879kf95c(v=vs.90).aspx and http://msdn.microsoft.com/en-us/library/vstudio/t32yf0a9(v=vs.100).aspx
http://msdn.microsoft.com/en-us/library/4z6b5d42(v=vs.110).aspx

Performing steps similar to the ones found at these URLs will display or hide a website image depending on whether or not the user has permissions to view it. See the .NET Errors section if errors occur. Some modifications may be needed to get this working.

A) If needed, enable or install the following tools. The first two can be installed under Control Panels, Programs, Add Program in Windows 7.

- Add Internet Information Services
- Add SMTP services

- Install SQL Server Express from See http://www.microsoft.com/en-us/server-cloud/products/sql-server-editions/sql-server-express.aspx for additional info.

The https://www.youtube.com/watch?v=vxxFhGF-Z7E youtube tutorial also provides a decent walkthrough for setting up the asp.NET tables and using them to assign user permissions and roles.

The http://msdn.microsoft.com/en-us/library/aa478948.aspx websites discuss membership services at a higher level and provides some PDF tutorials. The information below provides a quick summary from a tutorial on this website. Memorize all of these terms and you will be a hit at the next aspnet membership services party! ☺

Active Directory

Active Directory defines and maintains users, groups and security at the company or the enterprise level. See Active Directory under General Programming. Membership Services provide interface tools that work with Active Directory. These tools can be referenced under the system.web.security namespace within the .NET Framework.

Aspnet_Membership_CreateUser

This procedure is used to pull and push data from and into the membership database.

ASPState Tables

These tables provide information about the state of current user accounts and sessions. For instance the ASPStateTempSessions provides data related to temporary expired session. Some procedures that work with these tables include:

SQLSessionStateStore.DoGet
SQLSessionState.CreateTempTables
SQLSessionState.TempGetAppID
SQLSessionState.TempUpdateStateItemShortNullLong

AuthorizationStoreRoleProvider

The AuthorizationStoreRoleProvider class provides XML based Membership Services. This contains methods such as Create Role and Delete Role to perform role related tasks.

AZMan Data Store

This class provides XML based Membership Services.

BuildSiteMap

BuildSiteMap works with the XMLSiteMapProvider to create a Site Map of a users permissions in a related data source. It uses a GetConfigDocument helper method and an OnConfigFileChange handler to check for changes and refresh mappings.

InProcSessionStateStore

This is a type of State Provider. State refers to current user or computer values and settings associated with an application or a system.

Machine.config

Machine.config is a configuration file that will need information such as the data source in order to connect to the Membership Database.

OutOfProcSessionStateStore

This is a type of state provider.

Session State Provider

The Session State Povider provides the current state information of user account sessions using an InProcSessionStateStore, OutOfProcSessionStateStore, or a SqlSessionStateStore customized session store.

SqlConnectionHelper

This is a tool used to setup an SQL Express Database.

SQL Mail Health Monitoring Events

These events are used to inform an administrator when things occur within a system. A BufferedWebEventProvider class is used to log, respond to, diagnose, and forward web events. A processEvent processes the connections string looking at information like the EventID, EventTime, EventType, EventSequence, and Details from the aspnet_webevents_events table. The aspnet_webevent_logevent stored procedure is used to record the web events in the table.

SQL Membership DB

The SQL Membership DB is a DB containing user memberships. These providers are located under the system.web.security namespace within the .NET Framework.

SQLMembershipProvider

This class file is used to:

a. Initializing properties, read the connectionstring, check account properties, and throw exceptions.
b. Store information like the User Id and Password, Creation Date, and Email address.
c. Provide procedures and methods such as aspnet_Membership_CreateUser, aspnet_Membership.DeleteUser, aspnet_Membership_FindUsersByName, aspnet_Membership_Reset_Password, SqlMembershipProvider, ValidateUser, and MembershipPasswordFormat.Encrypted.

SQLProfileProvider

Thr SQLProfileProvider is a DB containing user profiles. These providers are located under the system.web.security namespace within the .NET Framework. In the DB, the aspnet_profile table includes information like the UserID, PropertyNames, and LastUpdatedData.

Some of the Stored Procedures used to access this data include aspnet_profile_deleteinactiveprofiles, aspnet_profile_getprofiles, and aspnet_profile_setproperties. The SetPropertyValues method is used to set profile information in the table and the GetPropertyValue method is used to retrieve the profile information.

The SQLSessionStateStore is a type of State Provider: Here is a list of some of the functionality it provides:

SetAndReleaseItemExclusive: A method used to serialize
    session state data
SQLSessionStateStore.ReleaseItemExclusive: A method used
    to releases any locks on session state data.
SQLSessionStateStore.SetAndReleaseItemExclusive.GetConnection:
A method used to setup a DB connection to session state data.
TempInsertStateItemLong: A method used to insert session state data.

<u>System.Web.Profile</u>

This namespace contains classes like the ProfileProvider class that will write and read data from the profile services in ASP.NET. Several methods in this class include DeleteProfiles, DeleteInactiveProfiles, GetAllProfiles, and FindProfilesByUserName. Some ProfileProvider properties include UserName and IsAuthenticated.

<u>System.Security</u>

The System.Security namespace contains classes like the MembershipProfiler that allows users to do things like Creating and DeletingUsers, Getting Passwords, and Enabling Password Retrieval. The procedures there are able to return requested information like Application Names and whether or not the system requires a Question and Answer for login purposes.

System.Web.Security

This namespace contains classes like the RoleProvider and the XMLSiteMapProvider. The RoleProvider class is responsible for providing the following functionality:

a. Role provision via methods such as the IsUserInRole, GetRolesForUser, CreateRole, andDeteleRole.
b. Role provider initialization, and caching of connection string information.
c. Mappings of applications, roles, and role names in the aspnet_roles table.
d. Mappings of users and roles in the aspnet_usersinroles table.
e. Stored procedures and methods such as aspnet_Roles_CreateRole, apsnet_Roles_GetAllRoles, aspnet_UsersInRoles_RemoveUsersFromRoles, Roles.AddUserToRole, and Roles.RemoveUsersToRole

System.Web.SessionState

This namespace contains classes like the SessionStateStoreProviderBase and SetAndReleaseItemExclusive. The SessionStateStoreProviderBase class provides methods like GetItem, SetAndReleaseItemExclusive, GetItemExclusive, and GetConnection (for initialization purposes). The SessionStateStoreProviderBase also supports items like Cookies and Cookieless Sessions through the use of methods like the CreateUninitializedItem and TempInsertUninitializedItem.

The SQLSessionStateStore class is used to store data in the ASPStateTempSessions table. This table contains information like the Session Ids, LockDates, and Timeout. The ASPTempStateApplications table links with the ASPStateTempSession to provide information specific to the ASP related App.

System.Web.UI.WebControls.WebParts

This namespace is used with Web Part controls and includes classes like the PersonalizationProvider and SQLPersonzliationProvider. The PersonalizationProvider class in the namespace is used to give layout and content information for the personalization of Web Parts.

Read about Web Parts under the MS SharePoint section in this book. The aspnet_personalizationallusers table stores Web Part personalized information. The aspnet_paths table stores path information for the application. Some stored procedures associated with the Personalization Provider include:
aspnet_PersonalizationAdministration_DeleteAllState,
aspnet_PersonalizationAdministration_GetCountOfState,
aspnet_PersonalizationPerUser_ResetPageSettings, and
aspnet_PersonalizationPerUser_SetPageSettings.
The SQLPersonalizationProvider.SavePersonalizationBlob procedure saves personalization information in the tables.
SqlPersonalizationProvider.aspnet_PersonalizationPerUser_GetPageSettings will read or get information from the tables.

XMLSiteMapProvider

This class provides A secure Mapping of User Site access. See System.Web.Security. These providers are located under the system.web.security namespace within the .NET Framework.

Case Study 3

MySQL and LINQ:

The previous Cast Study introduced the reader to membership services and .NET security. The following Case Study will discuss setting up a combo box using MySQL Client and LINQ technology.

To develop a simple Windows Form Application with a combo box using the MySQL Client library, a developer will perform steps similar to the ones described below.

1. http://www.dotnetperls.com/sqlconnection
2. http://social.msdn.microsoft.com/Forums/en-US/4ac1586b-0560-460a-a546-231d7cc627ca/how-to-fill-items-to-combobox-from-database-at-form-load-using-linq-to-sql-in-vbnet-?forum=linqtosql
3. http://social.msdn.microsoft.com/Forums/en-US/9387c998-3373-4d58-85dc-87bb9234e108/how-to-fill-combo-box-from-database-using-c?forum=csharplanguage
4. http://stackoverflow.com/questions/15651466/add-item-to-combobox-from-sql-query

1. http://msdn.microsoft.com/en-us/library/bb386951(v=vs.110).aspx explains how to create a multiple table selection.

Caste Study 4

Web Parts:

Web Parts are used in a Portal to provide enterprise related list and table information. This information can come from a variety of places like the REST and SOAP protocols or the Business Data Connectivity model.

Take a look at walkthroughs located at http://www.codeguru.com/csharp/.Net/net_asp/webforms/article.php/c12293/Write-Custom-WebParts-for-SharePoint-2007.htm to learn how to set up a Web Part using ASP.NET and C# technology.

Case Study 5

Report Builder:

This case study discusses developing reports with the Report Builder.

The .NET Report Builder tool is useful for developing filtered reports that can be run and viewed within a .NET application. Visit the following website to see steps for working with Report Builder: http://msdn.microsoft.com/en-us/library/dd255273.aspx

Case Study 6

Creating an Entity Data Model using the Entity Framework 6:

XSD stands for XML Schema Definition and .NET is able to create an XSD of a subset or an entire DB using a wizard. The developer is then able to use this to select, update, and delete data from the underlying objects located in the DB. http://www.asp.Net/mvc/tutorials/getting-started-with-ef-using-mvc/creating-an-entity-framework-data-model-for-an-asp-net-mvc-application is a good walkthrough for creating an entity data model. The following youtube tutorial also offers an explanation for how to accomplish this task:

https://www.youtube.com/watch?v=aj725vxlt9I

Case Study 7

Creating a Setup File:

In order to install the .NET application for one or more users the company may need a Windows installer project. To create a Windows Installer project example following the walkthrough steps at http://msdn.microsoft.com/en-us/library/cc656819(v=vs.90).aspx.

.NET Errors

The following is an overview of common .NET Errors a developer might run into using the .NET IDE. Possible solutions are provided along with the error.

ASP.NET Errors

1. A network-related or instance-specific error occurred while establishing a connection to SQL Server.

Verify that the Connection information is correct and that the SQL DB has been configured correctly.

2. The type or namespace [namespace name] could not be found:

Related code will need to have the same namespace association.
See the following websites for addition information about this problem:
http://weblogs.asp.Net/joewrobel/archive/2008/02/03/web-profile-builder-for-web- application-projects.aspx
http://leedumon.com/blog/asp-net-profiles-inweb-application-projects

3. Content is not supported outside the script or asp.content regions:

If the master page file was removed add a new one to reenter it in the web.config:

See http://stackoverflow.com/questions/2642132/error-with-masterpage for details on how to solve this problem.

4. Keyword not supported: 'Provider'.

The developer will need to supply the provider in the sqlDataSource key.

5. Only one top level element is allowed in an XML document.

See
http://forums.asp.Net/t/1688226.aspx?Only+one+top+level+element+is+allowed+in+an+XML+document for detail on how to resolve this.

1. ASP.NET 4.0 has not been registered.

Right click the command prompt and open it as Administrator and run C:\Windows\Microsoft.Net\Framework\v4.0.30319\apsnet_regiis –i
The command may change depending on the version of the Framework.

2. Could not load file or assembly 'MySql.Web, Version=6.7.4.0, Culture = neutral, PublicKeyToken=c5XXXXXXXX' or one of its dependencies.

To correct this error, uninstall MySQLConnector 6.7.X, and install version 6.6.6 or another 6.6 version that will work correctly with .NET.

3. Various Web Service Errors such as Error: Web Page Blocked.

A firewall device or software may be blocking content from a server. If this occurs, contact the network administrator to determine if this is the case.

The reader should also take a look at http://www.tutorialspoint.com/csharp/csharp_exception_handling.htm for a great overview of handling exceptions in the C# language.

Additional .NET Topics

Deserialize

This does not refer to the breaking of a morning cereal habit. ☺
This is the process of taking many data parts in a serialized string and assigning them to individual variables within the code. Serialized data could consist of a few fields or an entire XML schema representation with field values. See Serialize under General Programming.

Data Set

This terminology is not .NET specific. In this context it is a set of organized data that resides in the .NET memory cache. If the application needs to pull a filtered selection of data, store it, and update it, a data set is an ideal tool to utilize.

See http://msdn.microsoft.com/en-us/library/system.data.dataset.aspx for additional information.

REST

Learning about REST will not necessarily make life more relaxing. ☺
REST stands for Representational State Transfer. This protocol defines architectural tags and structures used to encase the characteristics and values of Data Sets within the world wide web and pass the information from one place to another. REST and JSON are becoming the preferred method for passing data back and forth between systems. Read Amazon Web Services for Dummies and for additional information. Also see REST under General Programming.

SOAP

This protocol will not make a developer cleaner. He or she will need to actually leave the computer and take a bath to accomplish that. ☺

Simple Object Access Protocol is a protocol used to exchange data from one place to another. It uses protocols like the Simple Mail Transfer Protocol and Hypertext Transfer Protocol Secure Socket Layer to transmit the information from point A to point B. Read

Programming Web Services with SOAP by O'Reilly Media for additional information on this topic. Read Amazon Web Services for Dummies and http://en.wikipedia.org/wiki/SOAP for additional information. Also see REST under General Programming.

Xamerian

Xamerian is a .Net Framework specification that allows developers to leverage tools like XAML in order to define things like page layout properties for various systems. Some of these systems include the MAc and iPhone.

XAML

The eXtensible Application Model Language uses XML technology to interact with the Windows Presentation Foundation in order to define layout features for an application or web page.

Database Technology

In this chapter:

1. **Concepts**
2. **Database SQLCommands**
3. **Database Objects**
4. **Data Types**
5. **Users And Roles**

Concepts

Databases contain tables and other objects used for storing, analyzing, and manipulating data. The following section will help the student to understand some of the concepts needed when working with a DB.

Checking Single Quotes

Selecting or filtering data with single quotes can be a tricky business. Most SQL tools see a single quote and attempt to examine the contents inside, i.e. Where deptno Like '123%'. If the developer wants to look up something like Phillip's Garage, he or she will need to do something like this: SELECT * FROM companies WHERE name = 'Phillip''s Garrage'. This lets SQL know that a single quote is being looked for.

In Oracle, if the developer wants to see what the SQL is actually looking for, he or she can Declare an anonymous block and then use a dbmsoutput.putline to return the statement. Here is an example:

Example: Run the following in an Oracle DB to declare an anonymous block and to examine the content of an SQL select statement stored in a variable in SQL Plus. The second statement shows how this can be achieved with Microsoft SQL Server. The statement can be run as an SQL statement to see if it is correct.

```
Set Verify Off;
Set ServerOutput On Size 100000;
Set linesize 300;
BEGIN
```

```
 DECLARE
  vMyQuery  VARCHAR2(2000);
 BEGIN
    vMyQuery := 'SELECT DISTINCT name FROM companies
           WHERE name = ''Phillip''''s Garage'' and zipcode = ''22222''';
     DbmsOutput.PutLine(vMyQuery);
  END;
END;
```

```
Begin

Declare @query Varchar(2000);

  Set @query = 'SELECT DISTINCT name FROM companies
           WHERE name = ''Phillip''''s Garage'' and zipcode = ''22222''';

  Print @query;

End;

End;
```

Choosing A Database

Remember Politics, Power, and Project. Politics plays a role in what DB a company uses. If a manager has family members working at Microsoft he or she may want to go with SQL Server. If ninety percent of the staff has Oracle experience he or she may want to select the Oracle DB. The Pharmaceutical industry will sometimes go with Oracle or .NET depending on the staff and the same situation exists in the electronic industry. The Public Safety sector generally uses .NET.

There are times when one product can deliver something the other one cannot. For instance, SQL Server developers can update a single table via an update statement that relates more than one table together.

One websites claims that Microsoft has a better support community. [1] Oracle claims to have better availability and less downtime compared to Microsoft. [2]

1. http://www.infoworld.com/d/data-management/real-difference-between-sql-server-and-oracle-755
2. http://www.oracle.com/technetwork/database/availability/ha-oracle12c-sqlserver2012-2049933.pdf

So, the right tool for the job also depends on what a company believes, what it wishes to achieve, and what it is selling. Managers will need to choose the most powerful tool suited for the project they are building.

Cursors:

Oracle DB:

The website and book references 1 and 2 below were used as the sole resources for the Oracle DB cursor explanations that follow them. The code has been modified to avoid plagiarism.

1. http://plsql-tutorial.com/plsql-explicit-cursors.htm

2. Technology Framers, Introduction To PL/SQL Programming, Version 3.4.4, Technology Framers, LLC.
1997-2001 p 3-3 through 3-21

Explicit Cursors:

These cursors require the user to declare, open, fetch, and close the cursor during its use. Here are a few code chunks to explain the process more intimately:

```
DECLARE
CURSOR employee_cur IS
SELECT empno, empname
FROM employees
WHERE department = 'HUMAN RESOURCES';
```

```
OPEN [the name of the cursor]
```

FETCH [the name of the cursor] INTO [the name of the record]
CLOSE [the name of the cursor]

Implicit Cursors:

Implicit cursors such as SELECT [data] INTO or SQL%ROWCOUNT process data or relay information without a lot of input from the developer. See the following examples for additional information:

SQL%ROWCOUNT
SQL%ROW_NUMBER
SQL%FOUND

SQL Server:

The book below was used as the sole resource for the SQL Server cursor explanations that follow:

1. Robert Vieira, SQL Server 2005 Programming, Wiley Publishing Inc., 2007 p. 434-450

Dynamic Cursor:

These cursors keep track of changes occurring within the DB.

Fast Forward Cursor:

AKA the Firehose Cursor, this cursor will loop through one record at a time, providing the application a read only format for each record.

Keyset Driven Cursors:

These cursors can be used to update data without affecting the data added after cursor invocation.

Static Cursor:

A static cursor pulls data that will not change. It is a view only shot of the data. To implement this functionality Developers declare a cursor in their package, open the cursor, and fetch the records. The following shows some code snippets for using a static cursor:

DECLARE [cursor name] GLOBAL STATIC FOR Select empno, name FROM employees;
OPEN [cursor name] FETCH NEXT FROM [cursorname] INTO @vEmpNo, vEmpName

DB Link:

A DB link allows an admin or developer to connect to another DB and use the objects there as if they existed in the current DB.

Flashback:

If you ever accidently step on a code change you can flashback oracle's source table: For example I restored a package body when I stepped on a change I made during the day: prereq: grant flashback on source$ to atscbs

get obect_id for the source code needing recovery.

select object_id from dba_objects where owner='CISCONVERT'

and object_name='DAFFRON_CONVERT_AR';

get the code using that object_id:

select SOURCE from sys.source$ as of timestamp to_timestamp('10-OCT-2016 07:00:00','DD-Mon-YYYY hh24:MI:SS')

where obj#=179170 ;

The code will have to cleaned up to be compiled but that can be done in textpad. Chris Naused 10/10/2016.

Inline View:

An Inline View is used with Microsoft SQL Server or an Oracle DB when filtering information from a variety of tables and then treating that selection as if it is a table in the FROM statement.

Example:

```
SELECT DISTINCT c.company_id,
                inline_view.product_id
FROM companies c,
        (SELECT o.company_id,
                o.date,
                d.product_id
        FROM orders o,
                details d
        WHERE o.order_master_id = d.order_master_id) inline_view
WHERE c.company_id < 5
        AND inline_view.company_id =c.company_id;
```

Tip:

Line up SQL code and align column names so that queries are easy to read. Some DB tools like PL/SQL Developer and Toad can "beautify" a query using tool menu selections.

Hosts:

Depending on the developers OS the Hosts file maybe located at C:/Windows/System32/drivers/etc/Hosts. It is used to map a group of host names to their IP addresses. If a developer is having trouble connecting to an application it may be related to a missing entry in this file. [1]

1. http://en.wikipedia.org/wiki/Hosts_(file)

Joins

When a developer has more than one table in a FROM statement, he or she can use joins to link the tables together. Some joins include LEFT, LEFT OUTER, LEFT INNER, RIGHT, RIGHT OUTER, and RIGHT INNER. Here are a few examples to make things clearer:

FROM employees e LEFT JOIN sales s ON s.empid = e.empid

This means to pull the selected fields (not shown) from these two tables where every record will be pulled from employees and only related records will be pulled from sales. Oracle developers can alternatively include employees e and sales s in the FROM clause and then use the e.empid (+)= s.empid statement in the WHERE clause.

FROM employees e RIGHT JOIN sales s ON s.empid = e.empid

This means to pull the selected fields (not shown) from these two tables where every record will be pulled from sales and only related records will be pulled from employees. Oracle developers can alternatively include employees e and sales s in the FROM clause and then use the e.empid = s.empid (+) statement in the WHERE clause.

Read through some of the basic DB books to obtain additional information regarding table joins.

Locks:

When two or more people are working with a table running selects and updates and inserts and deletes the DB may try to lock the table so that only one person can manipulate it at one time to avoid confussion. If this happens you can use the following to identify the locks:

```
SELECT L.SESSION_ID, S.USERNAME, S.OSUSER,
O.OBJECT_NAME, L.MODE_HELD
  FROM DBA_LOCKS L, DBA_OBJECTS O, V$SESSION S
 WHERE O.OBJECT_ID = L.LOCK_ID1
   AND L.SESSION_ID = S.SID
```

Use this website for additional information:
http://www.dba-oracle.com/t_find_oracle_locked_objects.htm

MySql:

MySql is a DB that can be downloaded and installed for free. The download can be found on the Internet at http:/www.mysql.com/downloads. The commands are SQL based. Many Internet applications run off of MySql technology. The following script will walk the reader through creating a few simple MySQL tables using the command line tool and will provide steps for how to load the tables using insert statements.

```
Mysql –u [the username from the installation] –p [the password]

CREATE DATABASE student;

SHOW DATABASES;

USE student;

CREATE TABLE IF NOT EXISTS students (
    studentid MEDIUMINT NOT NULL AUTO_INCREMENT
    student_firstname VARCHAR(50) NOT NULL,
    student_lastname VARCHAR(50) NOT NULL,
    student_dob DATE NOT NULL,
```

```
    student_address VARCHAR(50) NOT NULL,
    student_program VARCHAR(20) NOT NULL,
    student_marital_status INT(2) NOT NULL,
    student_country VARCHAR(20) NOT NULL,
    PRIMARY KEY (studentid)
) type=innodb;

ALTER TABLE students AUTO_INCREMENT = 5;

INSERT INTO students VALUES(
'Jonah','Smith','1969-07-08',
'4 1st Street', 'Computers', 'S','US');

INSERT INTO students VALUES(
'Mary','Cross','1969-03-01',
'2 2nd Street', 'Computers', 'S','US');

CREATE TABLE IF NOT EXISTS teachers (
    teacherid VARCHAR(7),
    teacher_firstname VARCHAR(50) NOT NULL,
    teacher_lastname VARCHAR(50) NOT NULL,
    teacher_dob DATE NOT NULL,
    teacher_address VARCHAR(50) NOT NULL,
    teacher_program VARCHAR(20) NOT NULL,
    teacher_marital_status INT(2) NOT NULL,
    teacher_country VARCHAR(20) NOT NULL,
    PRIMARY KEY (teacherid)
) type=innodb;

INSERT INTO teachers VALUES(
'1','Larry','Slate','1950-01-01',
'5 5th Street', 'Computers', 'S','US');

CREATE TABLE IF NOT EXISTS outliers(
    outlierid INTEGER(10) NOT NULL AUTO_INCREMENT
    studentid VARCHAR(7),
    teacherid VARCHAR(7),
    outliergrade VARCHAR(30),
    averagrade VARCHAR(30),
        PRIMARY KEY (outlierid),
```

```
    FOREIGN KEY (studentid) REFERENCES student(studentid),
    FOREIGN KEY (teacherid) REFERENCES teacher(teacherid)
  ) type=innodb;

ALTER TABLE outliers ADD UNIQUE INDEX (outlierid);

COMMIT;
```

Mysql developers should also be aware that a SQL Loader file can be used to insert records. For instance, to load data into the outliers table the user would create a c:/mysql/sqlldr/outlier.txt file that looks like this:

```
3,Jonah Smith,Larry Slate,7900,8000
4,Mary Cross,Larry Slate,8500,8000
```

Once the outliers text file has been created the user would use the command below to load the file:

```
LOAD DATA LOCAL INFILE 'c:/mysql/sqlldr/outliers.txt'
INTO TABLE outliers FIELDS TERMINATED BY ','
LINES TERMINATED BY '\r\n';

SELECT * FROM outliers;
```

ODBC:

An Open Oracle DB Connection can be setup in Control Panel – Data Sources. This driver allows Oracle Applications to login to a DB with a predefined connection specification. Note that these drivers can present a security concern when developers use them for things like creating a back door connection to an MS Access DB.

Object Oriented Databases:

An Object Oriented DB creates objects such as a person with a first and last name and an address with a street number, city, and state, and then uses those objects to create a table. The developer creates functions that will work with the objects to modify the data in specific ways. 1

1. Pinnacle Software Solutions, Inc Project Team, Project Support, and Administration staff, Oracle Fundamentals, elementk Press., 2000 p. 203-220

Persistence:

See Materialized View.

PL/SQL Developer:

PL/SQL Developer is developed and sold by Allround Automations. The tool is used to navigate through, modify, and beautify objects within an Oracle Database. Statement execution history is stored and users are allowed to lock and post records before a commit ever occurs. The tool allows Administrators to maintain Session level security. Developers can use it to navigate through DB objects such as a procedure using the Declaration, Function, Code Section, If, and Statement tabs in the SQL window. Go to www.allroundautomations.com/plsqldev.html to find out more about this useful tool.

Tips:

Use websites like http://www.williamrobertson.net/documents/plsqldeveloper-setup-1.html to set your configurations up. It is useful to learn how to use the Tools – Find option in PL/SQL Developer. This allows users to search for a regular expression within a subset of objects located within the current DB.

When using a tool like PL/SQL Developer try to keep as few windows open as possible and learn to use the Window menu bar to move back and forth between the windows.

RDBMS:

RDBMS stands for Relational Database Management System. It is a more descriptive name for some of the contemporary DB Systems.

Fine Grained Access:

Fine Grained Access allows a developer or DBA to audit table data changes at the row level.

Example:

The following demonstrates how to implement FGA in an Oracle Database.

```
--Turn on the auditing.
AUDIT SELECT, UPDATE, DELETE
ON schema_name.table_name
   BY DEFAULT WHENEVER SUCCESSFUL;

--See what is being audited.
SELECT object_name, policy_column
FROM dba_audit_policies
WHERE object_schema='schema_name';

--View the audits.
SELECT * FROM dba_fga_audit_trail ORDER BY
timestamp desc;
```

Pipelined Function:

See
https://asktom.oracle.com/pls/asktom/f?p=100:11:::::P11_QUESTION_ID:19481671347143

These let you treat a function as a table. So users can select from and modify data using statements like select * from plsql_Func.

PrimaryKey Constraint:

The PK ensures that the key identifier field for a table can be used to uniquely identify each table record. It can also be used to create a search Index making it easier to select data and update records.

Recordset:

In this context a record set is Microsoft Access specific. It is a set of organized data that resides in the Access application. If the application needs to pull data from the DB, loop through it, and modify the content, this is an ideal tool to use. See http://msdn.microsoft.com/en-us/library/system.data.dataset.aspx for additional information.

Regular Expressions:

Regular Expressions can be used to look for character and number sequences in various patterns. See Regular Expressions in the General Programming chapter of this book.

Example:

In an Oracle DB the developer can use reg_explike to do regular expressions searches as explained at http://docs.oracle.com/cd/B19306_01/appdev.102/b14251/adfns_regexp.htm.
To search for all records that have any amount of numbers in front and then any amount of non digits at the end an Oracle developer might use the following statement:

```
SELECT * FROM project_status WHERE
regexp_like(LOWER(projectid_display),'\d+\D+');
```

.NET uses Regex.IsMatch to check for regular expressions. See http://msdn.microsoft.com/en-us/library/3y21t6y4(v=vs.110).aspx for extended help on this topic.

Many regular expression testers can be found on the Internet. These tools allow users to test their expressions and verify they are working. The one at www.myregextester.com is one example. See Regular Expressions under General Programming for additional informaiton.

Required Field:

This is a field in a table that must have a value (it cannot be NULL) when it is inserted or updated. It could be required at the form level. However, requiring it at the table level ensures the requirement is never overlooked.

Source:

The Oracle Source table has entries for and can be used to examine all of the objects in every schema within a DB.

SQL:

SQL is the language most commonly used to maintain DB information. The Standard Query Language consists of four sub-languages:

Data Control Language: Used to Grant and Revoke permissions.

Example:

This example grants and revokes select privileges to a table for a user.

GRANT SELECT ON "SCHEMA_NAME"."TABLE_NAME" TO "USER_NAME";

REVOKE SELECT ON "SCHEMA_NAME"."TABLE_NAME" FROM "USER_NAME";

Data Definition Language: Used to Create, Alter, and Drop objects.

Tip:

Mixing up a Revoke command with the more permanent Drop User command is useful when a developer does not like his or her career. ☺

Data Manipulation Language: Used to Select, Update, Insert, and Delete data.

Transaction Control Language: Used to set Savepoints, Rollback changes, or Commit data changes.

Tip:

Use statements like the Oracle DB Savepoint and Rollback and Commit to undo or save work. Take note that a rollback statement can not be issued after a DCL or DDL command has been run.

Example:

This example will set a Savepoint and then undo all the statements in Set 2.

[Some DML SQL Statements (Set 1)]

Savepoint [Savepoint Name];

[Some DML SQL Statements (Set 2)];

Rollback [Savepoint Name];

Commit; --Saves (Set 1).

SendMail:

This Oracle PL/SQL package or a similar module is used by a DB to connect to and send mail from a mail server. SendMail is available to download and can be located using a simple search on the Internet.

SQL Plus:

The SQL Plus command line interface tool can perform most of the operations PL/SQL Developer and Toad can but it does not have the Graphical interface. It also uses fewer resources. That feature can be nice when using commands like desc to describe a table or running a simple check using a statement like the one below. A plugin is needed in order to use this tool with Microsoft SQL Server.

```
--Use a simple check to determine if a procedure returns True or False
Set ServerOutput On;
DECLARE

BEGIN

 IF PackageName.Procedure('True') THEN
   dbms_output.put_line('Procedure Returned True');
 Else
   dbms_output.put_line('Procedure Returned False');
 End If;

END;
```

Subquery:

A subquery is used when a developer pulls a single field value at the row level that is selected from a table using a specified criteria. Notice the last line where the e.deptno equals NVL(&pDeptNo, e.deptno). This means if a value exists in the &pDeptNo parameter filter on it and, if not, the deptno will equal itself and this filter will be ignored.
An example of a subquery:

```
SELECT e.employee_id,
       e.employee_name,
      (SELECT SUM(o.amount)
       FROM orders o
```

```
        WHERE o.employee_id = e.employee_id)
          Employee_Order_Amount
FROM employees e
WHERE e.active = 'Y'
        And e.deptno = NVL(&pDeptno,e.deptno);
        --See the notes above regarding NVL.
```

Synonym:

A synonym creates an alias for a DB object. A synonym can be used so that users can select and manipulate an object in another DB schema as if it exists in the current DB schema.

Example:

The following example demonstrates the creation of a synonym.

```
CREATE SYNONYM employees FOR mystore.employees;
```

Tip:

It is usually necessary to grant synonym permissions to a role or individual users for the user(s) to be able to properly access an object. Take a look at the Grant command under the Data Control Language in the SQL section above.

T-SQL:

Transact-SQL is used to perform SQL commands with Microsoft products such as .NET.

Toad:

Toad can be used with Microsoft SQL Server or an Oracle DB. It offers many options for looking at the data. Developers can beautify their code, tune for performance, and locate objects easily using this tool. See www.software.dell.com/Toad-For-Oracle or www.quest.com for additional information.

Updating a Single Table Via A Multiple Table Selection:

This is an awesome feature that Microsoft SQL Server provides. The following demonstrates a simple example for how to accomplish this.

```
UPDATE employees, emp_sales_totals
   SET employees.needs_raise = 'Y'
WHERE employees.emp_id = emp_sales_totals.emp_id
         AND emp_sales_total.value > 100000;
```

XML Database:

Oracle allows developers to create an XML based Database with XML based tables and objects. A unique set of commands are used to create, select from, and maintain these tables. Read more about this topic at http://docs.oracle.com/database/121/ADXDB/xdb03usg.htm#ADXDB4044.

Database SQL Commands

Coalesce:

This SQL command takes a large group of items and returns the first item in the list. For instance the following statement will return “a”.

```
SELECT COALESCE(‘a’,’b’,’c’) FROM dual;
```

DCL:

Read about the Data Control Language in the Concepts – SQL section of this chapter.

DDL:

Read about the Data Definition Language in the Concepts – SQL section of this chapter.

Decode:

The Decode command locates a string value and changes it as directed by the parameters.

Example:

The example below changes the string to ‘BRE’, ‘LUN’, or ‘DIN’ depending on the string value.

```
SELECT
DECODE(food_choice,'eggs','BRE','sandwitch','LUN','steak',
'DIN','Unknown')
FROM meals;
```

DML:

Read about the Data Manipulation Language in the Concepts – SQL section of this chapter.

Extend Segment Command:

DBAs or permitted developers may need to extend the memory segment for a database. This occurs when the DB uses more than the allotted amount of memory to perform requested tasks. Search for the extend segment command on the Internet or discuss this topic with a DBA for more details.

Intersect:

This command is used to determine the intersection of data between one or more tables. The select statements have to correspond with each other if a developer wants to insert this command between them.

Example:

Intersect shows employees making < $50000 who made > $50000 in company profits.

```
SELECT employee FROM employee
WHERE salary < 50000
INTERSECT
SELECT employee FROM
        (SELECT employee,
                SUM(profit)
         FROM sales
         GROUP BY employee
         HAVING SUM(profit) > 50000
        );
```

Tip: Use the Group By command to group records with similar data. Use the Having command to filter it.

Tip: A Vin Diagram can be useful to display intersecting information.

VIN Diagram Example

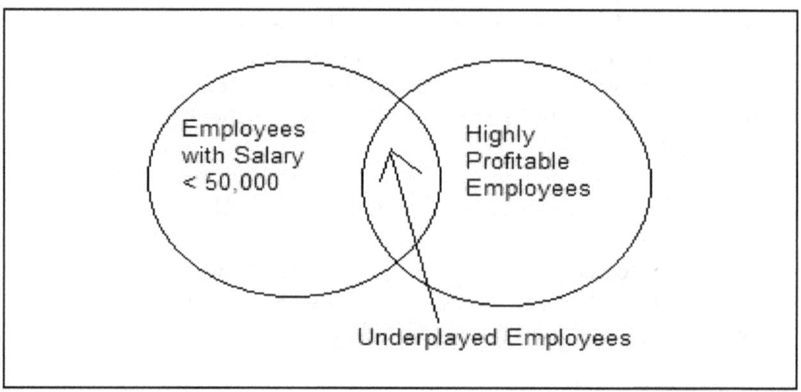

Minus:

Minus is used to remove a selection of table records from another set of table records. The select statements have to be the same in order to insert the minus command between them. See the Intersect example for a similar querying technique and an example.

NULL:

If a variable or table value is set to NULL it means it does not have a defined value. It is not 0 and it is not necessarily blank. The value is unknown so many applications have difficulty working with it.

Tip: Understanding the NULL value is important when dealing with other topics such as Form and Report Development as well.

Whether working in the DB or in an application, the code generally interprets this to be an unidentifiable value. So, in other words, if a developer is using a condition to determine if a variable is NULL the application may give incorrect or confusing results. It is highly recommended that developers use something like the NVL function to set NULL values to 0 or or something similar, so that they can add, subtract, multiply, divide, and manipulate these values consistently and correctly. NVL will take a field and substitute another value if it is NULL.

Example:

Use NVL(Field1,0) + NVL(Field2,0) as opposed to Field1 + Field2 when Field 1 or Field 2 may be NULL.

Lower:

Use this function to convert upper case characters in a string to lower case. Here is a selection example:

Example:

SELECT Lower('WIG') FROM dual; --The output will be wig.

LPAD:

Use this tool to add a specified number of characters or numbers (i.e. 0) to the left of a value.

Over (ORDER BY):

Group By will group records and then do a calculation on them for each record group. Partition by will determine an aggregate for a group and return that one value in each record that makes up the record group. Over will run an aggregate function over every record and return that value for every record unless the partition by statement is used to filter down to a smaller group of records.

For instance, if a developer calculates the Sum(retail_cost) Over () he or she will get the Overall Sum for the entire result of the records selected and it will return for every record in the table.

Example:

The following is an ORACLE DB example:

This example will first pull back all of the employee records with a salary greater than 40000. Then it will search for the first salary value within those record and return the minimum salary and employee combination for every record. A similar technique can be used with MS SQL Server.

```
SELECT department,
        firstname,
        lastname,
        salary,
        MIN(TO_CHAR(salary)||' '||firstname||'-'||lastname) OVER
        (ORDER BY salary) mv
FROM employee_records
WHERE salary > 40000;
```

Some Oracle DB aggregate functions include:

First_Value
Last_Value
Min
Max
Row_Number

Some Microsoft SQL Server aggregate functions include:

Avg
Count
Sum

http://msdn.microsoft.com/en-us/library/ms189461.aspx discusses these in greater detail

Tip:

Oracle DB and SQL Server have similar sets of aggregate functions. See Partition By for additional refinement.

See the following references for additional information:
1. http://stackoverflow.com/questions/2404565/sql-server-difference-between-partition-by-and-
2. http://www.midnightdba.com/Jen/2010/10/tip-over-and-partition-by/
There is a great example at:
3. https://asktom.oracle.com/pls/asktom/f?p=100:11:0::::P11_QUESTION_ID:122801500346829407

Partition By (ORDER BY):

See Over (ORDER BY) for an explanation. This filters down to a selected group and then pulls an aggregate for every record.

Example

This Oracle example will first pull all of the Employees with a Salary greater than $40,000. Then it will look through all the records associated with the current records department and determine the First Salary and employee combination and return that value for each of the related department records. A similar technique can be used with MS SQL Server.

```
SELECT department,
          firstname,
          lastname,
          salary,
          first_value(
   TO_CHAR(salary)||' '||firstname||'-'||lastname)
OVER (PARTITION BY department ORDER BY
department) firstSalary
FROM employee_records
WHERE salary > 40000;
```

Example

Use Partition By to find the latest position for a given employee.

```
create table employee_positions
(firstname varchar2(100),
 lastname varchar2(100),
 position varchar2(100)
);

insert into employee_positions
values
('John','Allen','Developer 1');
insert into employee_positions
values
('John','Allen','Developer 2');
insert into employee_positions
values
('Jim','Jones','Developer 1');
insert into employee_positions
values
('Ben','Smith','Developer 1');
insert into employee_positions
values
('Ben','Smith','Developer 2');
insert into employee_positions
values
('Ben','Smith','Developer 3');
commit;
select * from employee_positions;

--Go through the first and last name combinations
--and determine the latest employee position.
SELECT DISTINCT latest_position FROM
(
SELECT firstname ||' - '|| lastname || '-' || position latest_position,
position, max(position)
    OVER (PARTITION BY firstname, lastname) mp
FROM employee_positions
```

```
WHERE lastname IN ('Allen','Jones','Smith')
)
WHERE position = mp;

--The Group By alternative below is longer, messier, and slower.
SELECT DISTINCT empname ||' - '||
(SELECT DISTINCT position
FROM employee_positions
WHERE position = a.position and empname = a.empname) position
FROM
(
SELECT firstname || '-' || lastname empname,
MAX(position) position
FROM employee_positions
WHERE LOWER(lastname) IN ('allen','jones','smith')
GROUP BY firstname || '-' || lastname
) a

--The results are:
--Ben – Smith - Developer 3
--Jim – Jones - Developer 1
--John – Allen - Developer 2
```

Some Oracle DB aggregates functions include:

First_Value
Last_Value
Min

Max
Row_Number

Some Microsoft SQL Server aggregate functions include:
Avg
Count
Sum

1. http://msdn.microsoft.com/en-us/library/ms189461.aspx

Tip:

Oracle DB and SQL Server have similar sets of aggregate functions.

See Over for additional details.

Pivot:

The pivot function is very useful when dealing with columns that need to be displayed as rows or vice versa. For instance if an error log is used where the first column is the table name, the second column is the field name, and the third column is the field value etc, the developer will need to use something like the pivot function in Microsoft SQL or Oracle to pivot the values and analyze the data easier. When incorporating this term in the from clause the values in the columns specified will become the column headers in the result set.

Developers can find good examples of selecting data using the pivot functionality in the following locations:

Microsoft SQL Server:

http://technet.microsoft.com/en-us/library/ms177410(v=sql.105).aspx

Oracle DB:

http://www.oracle.com/technetwork/articles/sql/11g-pivot-097235.html
http://www.adp-gmbh.ch/ora/sql/examples/pivot.html

REPLACE:

This command replaces values with new values in the selected string.

Example:

This example removes all the dashes from a security number.

SELECT REPLACE(ssn, '-', '') FROM employees;

RPAD:

Use the RPAD tool to add a specified number of characters or numbers (ie. 0) to the right of a value.

Sqlldr:

This tool is used to load data from a delimited file into a DB table. See the MySQL section above.

Sync:

This command can be run for an Oracle DB to synchronize DB pieces or an entire DB Schema with another DB such as a testing DB.

SysDate:

This is the Current Date from the OS on the Server hosting the DB.

TCL:

Read about the Transaction Control Language in the Concepts – SQL section of this chapter.

To_Char:

To_Char will take a value (usually a number or date) and convert it into a character or string.

Tip:

Use TO_CHAR(vDateVariable, 'DAY') to convert dates to days.

To_Date

To_Date will take a string value and convert it to a date.

Tip:

In some Oracle Applications and or DB objects a developer can incorporate an Exception When Others clause to return a message if a value is not a proper date.

```
EXCEPTION

WHEN OTHERS THEN

--A message regarding the error.

END
```

Tip:

When comparing values like 1-Jan-2014 to 15-Jan-2014 it is important to use a TO_DATE. i.e. WHERE TO_DATE(1-Jan-2014) < TO_DATE(15-Jan-2014). If not the Database might think the application is comparing strings instead of dates.

Union:

The Union command will take two selected datasets and return every unique record. See Union All.

Example: The following will return each unique department and only one additional unique record without data.

```
(SELECT deptno
    FROM department
    UNION
    SELECT NULL deptno
        FROM department WHERE rownum < 19) ;
```

Union All:

Union All will take two selected datasets and return each record from the selection. See Union.

Example: The following will return each unique department and eighteen individual records without data.

```
(SELECT deptno
     FROM department
     UNION ALL
     SELECT NULL deptno
         FROM department WHERE
rownum < 19) ;
```

Upper:

Use the Upper function to convert lower case characters to upper case. Here is a selection example:

```
SELECT Upper('wig') FROM dual;
--The output will be WIG.
```

Variance:

Variance is s function used to see how much a value varies from the other selected values in a query result set.

Database Objects

Database System Tables

The following is a list of some of the useful Oracle tables:

All_Tab_Columns

This table is used to return information about all the table columns within a Database.

All_Tables

This table is used to return information about all the tables within a Database.

All_Functions

This table is used to return information about the functions available within a Database.

All_Indexes

This table is used to return information about the table indexes within a Database.

All_Procedures

This table is used to return information about the procedures available within a Database.

Dual

The dual table is used to pull a 1 column – 1 record value from the Database. Here are a few examples of using the dual table to pull information.

```
Select '1' from dual;
Select user from dual;
Select sysdate from dual;
```

Select userenv from dual;

Select 'My Column Name' MyColumnName from dual;
Select [SequenceName].NextVal from dual; [1]

1.
https://asktom.oracle.com/pls/asktom/f?p=100:11:0::::P11_QUESTION_ID:1562813956388

User_Source

This table can be used to examine all of the objects in a user schema within a Database.

The following is a list of some useful Microsoft SQL Server tables:

SysAlerts

This table lists any alerts setup in the Database. These alerts are used to inform the users and administrators if an unexpected event occurs.

SysColumns

This table lists the table columns within the Database.

SysConstraints

This table lists the table and column level constraints within the Database.

SysDatabases

This table lists the Databases created on the Server.

SysForeignKeys

This table lists the table column Foreign Key mappings within the Database.

SysJobSchedules

This table lists scheduled jobs. Developers can create Database level processes called Jobs that fire when specified.

SysIndexes

This table lists the table column level indexes set up within the Database. An index works like a phone directory for the Database so that table data can be retrieved and stored more efficiently.

SysLanguages

This table lists the various languages available within the Database.

CLOB:

CLOB is a Character Large Object. It is used to store large alphabetic symbols like various Chinese letters.

Constraint:

Table constraints are used to ensure that certain conditions are met before inserting table data. See the Foreign Key, Primary Key, and Required Field constraints below.

Container:

This terminology is Microsoft Access specific for the purposes of this book. It is a set of organized objects located in the Access application. Examples include Form and Report labels, Text Fields, and Combo Boxes. The user can use a for loop to traverse an enumeration of container items and then modify their properties. This is very helpful if, for example, a developer wants to change a single word throughout the DB. See http://msdn.microsoft.com/en-us/library/office/bb177484(v=office.12).aspx for additional information.

Example:

This container loop example shows a message box for each of the forms within the current Access DB:

```
'To set this up 1)  Create an Access form with a button.  2)  Go to
properties on the button.  3)  Add the following Event Click procedure.
4)  Run the form.
5)  Click the button.

Private Sub Command0_Click()
  Dim dbName As DAO.Database
  Dim doc As DAO.Document
  'Dim frmName As Form
  Dim ctrl As DAO.Container

Debug.Print "Start:"

  Set dbName = CurrentDb
  Set ctrl = dbName.Containers("Forms")

With dbName

    For Each doc In ctrl.Documents
      MsgBox (doc.Name)
      'frmName = doc.Name
    Next doc

    '.Close   Use if using OpenDatabases to check other DB objects

  End With
End Sub
```

Database Trigger:

These allow DBAs to run triggers such as login and exit triggers at the Database level.

DBLink:

A Database Link is used to link to a separate Database and reference and manipulate the objects in that Database.

Foreign Key Constraint:

This constraint ensures that data exists in another Database table before inserting it in a table row.

Index:

See Index under General Programming.

Materialized View:

This view resides on the Server disk and is updated at a specified time interval. The time interval is specified in the view definition.

Example:

Here is a Oracle DB example of a Materialized View that displays the Sum of every purchase amount that a specific sales employee is responsible for. The data refreshes every time the query is run.

```
CREATE MATERIALIZED VIEW view_name
BUILD DEFERRED
REFRESH COMPLETE ON DEMAND
AS
SELECT First_table.employee_name,
          SUM(Second_table.purchase_amount)

FROM First_Table,
         Second_Table
WHERE Second_table.employee_number =
First_table.employee_number;
```

Tip:

Materialized Views are called Indexed Views in Microsoft SQL Server.

Primary Key Constraint:

Adding this unique constraint to a table field ensures that it will uniquely identify each record.

Required Field Constraint:

Adding this constraint to a table field ensures that it must have a value. The value cannot be NULL.

Sequences:

See Sequence Issues.

Sequence Issues:

Sequences are usually used to generate a unique primary key within a table. They can be generated in increments of one or some other value. If a developer runs into errors that mention a sequence problem it could mean the sequence has not been created or it could mean he or she needs to move the last sequence number up so it is in sync with the last number in the table.

Example:

Here are a few example scenarios. The URLs numbered below each example provide additional references for these concepts.

Microsoft SQL Server:

```
Create Sequence SchemaName.SequenceName Start With 1
Increment By 1;
GO
```

Reference:
http://msdn.microsoft.com/en-us/library/ff878091.aspx

ALTER SEQUENCE SchemaName.SequenceName Restart With 100;

Reference:
http://msdn.microsoft.com/en-us/library/ff878572.aspx

Oracle DB:

```
CREATE SEQUENCE SchemaName.SequenceName
        START WITH 100
        INCREMENT BY 1
        NOCACHE
        NOCYCLE;
```

References:

1. http://docs.oracle.com/cd/B12037_01/server.101/b10759/statements_6014.htm
2. http://www.dba-oracle.com/t_oracle_nextval_function.htm

To restart the Sequence a developer will need to drop it and rerun the create sequence command.

Reference:
http://docs.oracle.com/cd/B19306_01/server.102/b14200/statements_2011.htm

Tip:

Many times developers will get errors related to the sequence number not being in sync - i.e. if a Unique table ID goes through the number 100 but the next sequence number is 99, the insertion may become blocked. This is because the 99th record is already in the table. In this situation a developer will need to increment the Sequence number or restart it at 101.

Triggers:

Triggers such as an after update or delete trigger fire and perform a series of commands when events occur for a Database object.

Be careful using triggers. For example, when creating a trigger that calls itself over again this can lead to ORA-04091 Table X is mutating. The OWA_UTL.WHO_CALLED_ME procedure can be used to determine who called the trigger and stop this problem before it occurs.

Data Types

Boolean:

This is a variable with a TRUE or FALSE value.

Dates:

Dates use the internal computer clock to determine a numeric offset and relate it to the user as a human comprehendible date and time. Microsoft and Oracle and other Databases use different techniques to record and select these values. The following is a list of some date selections from a Microsoft SQL Server DB and an Oracle DB. Study the references to discover additional information about dates.

Oracle DB:

```
--Search the table for a date:
SELECT TO_CHAR(date_column_name, 'MM/DD/RRRR') FROM
table_name WHERE TO_CHAR(date_column_name,
'MM/DD/RRRR') like '02/24/2012%';

 --Pull the year from the date in the selection:
SELECT EXTRACT(year FROM DATE '2013-01-20') FROM dual
ORDER BY 1 DESC;
```

Reference:
http://www.techonthenet.com/oracle/functions/extract.php

```
--Select the Max day of the week.
SELECT MAX(TO_CHAR(t.date_column_name,'D')) FROM
table_name t;

--Set the date value where the table id is 70.
UPDATE table_name set date_column = TO_DATE('09/30/2005
11:59:59 PM','MM/DD/YYYY HH:RR:SS PM') where id = 70;
```

Reference:
http://infolab.stanford.edu/~ullman/fcdb/oracle/or-time.html

--Select the date column in a specified format.
SELECT TO_DATE('May 02, 2014, 10:03:08 P.M.','Month dd, YYYY, HH:MI:SS P.M.', 'NLS_DATE_LANGUAGE = AMERICAN') FROM table_name;

Reference:
http://docs.oracle.com/cd/B14117_01/server.101/b10749/ch9sql.htm

--Trunc will truncate any date format to a DD-MON-YYYY.
--Additional format options are available with the parameters.
-- The following selection will return 8/12/14 on August 12th, 2014.
SELECT TRUNC(sysdate) FROM dual;

Microsof tSQL Server:

--Search the table for a date:
SELECT date_column_name FROM table_name WHERE date_column_name = '2010-04-01' ORDER BY date_column_name;

Reference:
http://stackoverflow.com/questions/10643379/how-do-i-query-for-all-dates-greater-than-a-certain-date-in-sql-server

--Pull the year from a date in the table:
SELECT DATEPART(yyyy, '1/10/2014') FROM dual;

Reference:
http://stackoverflow.com/questions/12436743/how-to-extract-only-the-year-from-the-date-in-sql-server-2008

--Select the Max day of the week using a date parameter.
SELECT MAX(DATEPART(dd, '1/10/2014')) FROM table_name t;

--Select the Current Date in a specified format.
--The following is an exact quote from the http://www.sql-server-helper.com/tips/date-formats.aspx. This website is a great guide for selecting dates from a DB with various formats.

SELECT CONVERT(VARCHAR(20), GETDATE(),110) AS [MM-DD-YYYY];

Tip:

These general concepts can be used when selecting, inserting, and updating dates. It is important to realize that dates are not stored in a computer the way we store them in our mind. Dates are stored in a computer as offset numbers representing the number of milliseconds that have passed from a specified point of time. When the year 2000 rolled around some platforms were not able to handle this offset. When running into problems dealing with dates developers should keep in mind that the underlying technology does a lot to translate these values on the back end.

Y2K Note:

Y2K issues refer to issues related to how to deal with the change from 19XX to 20XX. For instance, Oracle handles this issue by using a DD-MON-RRRR format mask for date values. However, if a 10 character date is stored in a string data type and the developer attempts to format this as DD-MON-RRRR that may present a problem in the future. This mask converts a string value of 01-Jan-50 to 01-Jan-1950, so if the user intends this to be 01-Jan-2050 he or she could be in for a surprise.

Decimal:

If a developer assigns an Oracle datatype of NUMBER(9,5) to a field this means 4 digits are possible in the integer piece of the number and 5 digits are possible in the decimal. So 1234.12345 is allowed, 1234 is allowed, .12345 is allowed, 12345 is not allowed and .123456 is not allowed. Also be aware that the Oracle FM9999.999 format will return values in every position as long as it is not a leading or trailing zero. FM0000.000 will display leading zeros and trailing zeros and FM9999.000 will display all the trailing zeros.

Example:

Checking numeric formatting can be difficult. When checking for numeric values with a specified value in Oracle Forms it might be necessary to create a When-Validate-Trigger to check each part of the number and verify that it is, in fact, numeric:

```
....

vNum := LENGTH(TRIM(TRANSLATE(:BLOCK.FIELD, '
+-.0123456789', ' '))); 1

SELECT
LENGTH(SUBSTR(:BLOCK.FIELD,1,INSTR(:BLOCK.FIE
LD,'.')-1)) INTO vBefore
  FROM dual;

SELECT
LENGTH(SUBSTR(:BLOCK.FIELD,INSTR(:BLOCK.FIEL
D,'.')+1,LENGTH(:BLOCK.FIELD))) INTO vAfter
  FROM dual;

IF vNum > 0 OR vBefore > 5 OR vAfter > 3 THEN
  Call_Alert('Failure','Please use this format: 99999.999.');
  :BLOCK.FIELD := NULL;
  RAISE Form_Trigger_Failure;
END IF;

...
```

Reference:
http://www.techonthenet.com/oracle/questions/isnumeric.php

Percents:

Different techniques are used to format DB values as a percentage of a whole. The following examples demonstrate the technique.

Oracle DB:

```
SELECT
REPLACE(TO_CHAR(percent_column_name,'999G999G999G999G9
90D00') || '%',' ','') percent_column_label FROM [table_name];
```

Reference:
http://www.asquestion.com/question/26628065531308397

SQL Server:

```
SELECT CAST(CAST(0.10*100 AS numeric(10,3)) AS varchar(6)) +
'%'  as pct_column_name
```

Reference:
http://www.sqlservercentral.com/Forums/Topic558696-338-1.aspx

---

Tip:

These values would be displayed in a character field such as a VARCHAR or a VARCHAR2 field in Oracle Developer Forms or a Java String or TextField in some other Applications.

Users And Roles

DBA:

The Database Administrator is responsible for maintaining functional Database platforms on which Database applications may be built. DBAs should be familiar with many of the Database tools mentioned in this chapter and especially this section.

DBLink:

A DB link is used to link to a separate Database and reference and make modifications to objects within that Database.

Foreign Key Constraint:

The foreign key constraint ensures that data exists in another Database table before inserting it into a table row.

Index:

See Index under General Programming.
Also see the MySQL section below.

Locks:

A lock occurs when two or more users are trying to modify an object like a table or record simultaneously. Various configurations will handle these locks differently and sometimes the entire system will lock up until the locks are released. An Oracle DBA or developer can select from the following Oracle tables, among others, to look for possible deadlock issues: v$process, v$parameter, v$session, and dba_scheduler_running_jobs. In order to release these locks an administrator will need to issue commands that will do things like altering the system, setting scheduler attributes, or stopping jobs.

The reader should take a look at the following Website Locations for additional information:

1. http://www.mssqltips.com/sqlservertip/2927/identify-the-cause-of-sql-server-blocking/
2. http://dev.mysql.com/doc/refman/5.0/en/innodb-deadlocks.html

Roles:

Roles are permission groupings that define what a User or Group of Users is permitted to do within the Database or a System.

Schema:

Data is stored in user schemas. Examples include the DB owner and a security schema. These schemas, in turn, are stored in table spaces on the Operating System. Synonyms are created to permit easy access to objects in one schema that were created and maintained in another.

Session:

When a User logs in, a Session is created to allow the user to access their permited DB objects until they log out. If an application is not logged out properly this can lead to locking and performance related issues. When this happens a DBA may need to "kill" the Session and make other adjustments. See Locks above.

Users:

See Session and Schema above.

Networking

In this chapter:

1. **Tools**
2. **Concepts**
3. **Computers, Devices, and Hardware**

Many programs are written to work with a computer network so it is important for programmers to have a moderate understanding of network architecture and similar principles. This will allow the developer to ensure their programs will continue to function with heavier traffic and other unforeseen issues that develop over time.

Tools

Active Directory:

Active Directory provides template information and network specifications for developing and maintaining a system of computers within an organization. Some organization examples include enterprises and large companies. Using this tool an administrator is allowed to create user groups with a permissible set of hardware devices and software applications. He or she is able to use these objects to customize who has access to what, at both group and individual levels. For instance the Microsoft Active Directory User Management tool allows a company to create users like managers, support technicians, and human resource personnel with the initial tools and access they will need when they log into their computer. Templates can also be setup that will be used to control what software and hardware is installed or available for these groups and individuals.

Reference:
John Kane, Mitchell Beaton, Merrick Van Dongen of Microsoft Learning, Custom Editorial Production, Inc., Jennifer Lartz, Michelin Fredrick, Kerry Weinstein, Harry Nolan, Michael St. Martine, and Lauren Sapira/Elena Santa Maria, Windows Server 2008 Active Directory Configuration, John Wiley & Sons, 2009, p. 1-289

Aperture:

This tool was developed by Apple. It allows a company to map out their entire infrastructure recording the location of lights, network boxes, computers, IP addresses etc. It is most useful for network engineers who need to locate pieces of equipment or other objects efficiently. See En.wikipedia.org/wiki/Aperture_(software) for additional details.

Cute FTP:

This is an FTP tool with a cuter look and feel. See SFTP.

DNS:

A Domain Name System server is used to resolve Internet IP addresses to character-based-names that can be read by humans like Amazon.com. Please excuse the incorrect English. This does not mean that Amazon.com is a human. ☺

Filezilla:

This is a free FTP utility used to transfer files from one place to another. See SFTP.

SFTP:

SFTP stands for Secure File Transfer Protocol. It uses encryption to move files back and forth between a Source and a Destination:

Uptime:

Uptime is used to determine the availability or uptime of a remote computer on the network.

VPN:

VPN stands for Virtual Private Network. VPN software is used to establish a secure and encrypted link between a remote computer and a host or network so the user can use the computer remotely.

Wireshark:

This free tool lets users see networking information like TCP/IP protocol commands, bits, and even data segments as it passes across the network.

Concepts

Checksum:

Protocols like Internet Protocol (IP) insert a Checksum value at the end of a data segment to alert the receiver if data changes as it is comes across the wire or other device.

CRC:

This stands for Cyclical Redundancy Check. It is common to use a networking algorithm to determine if data gets modified. The sender attaches a hidden numeric message inside the data. Then the receiver uses polynomial division on the message to determine if the data was changed.

Etc Hosts:

See Hosts in the Database chapter.

Network Topology:

Network Topology refers to the way a network is laid out and connected together. Here are some examples of Network Topologies.

Bus: A linear network topology.

Mesh: A topology where each computer is connected to several other computers or possibly every other computer.

Ring: A ring shaped topology.

Star: Every computer is connected to a central computer.

Tree: A topology with a root node.

Token Ring: A star or ring topology with a token that is used to alert the other computers if a problem occurs.

Socket:

This term is used a lot when networking in a Java Application. It is sometimes necessary to establish username, password, and a server port connection, AKA a Socket in order for the program to interact with an Application or Website on the Server. Read the "Java Creating A Secure Socket Example" in the Java chapter for additional information.

SSL:

Secure Socket Layer. See Socket above and the "Opening A Secure Socket" example under Java.

Subnet Mask:

This topic is very involved. The following is a very general explanation of what it does. When networking computers together, engineers can use different subnet masks to control what TCPIP addresses will be used with the domain controller and other servers and clients on the network. If a type A subnet mask is used then the computers will only resolve or use or map addresses within the first octet (8 bits) of the TCPIP address. If a type B subnet mask is used then the computer will only resolve or map addresses within the first two octets (8 bits) of the TCPIP address and so on.

See http://www.tcpipguide.com/free/t_IPDefaultSubnetMasksForAddressClassesABandC.htm for some additional information.

Class A: 255.0.0.0
11111111.00000000.00000000.00000000

Class B: 255.255.0.0
11111111.11111111.00000000.00000000

Class C: 255.255.255.0
11111111.11111111.11111111.00000000

Note that engineers use the Network and Sharing Center as well as the System – Computer Name – Network ID settings found under Control Panel on some Windows based computers to set subnetting properties.

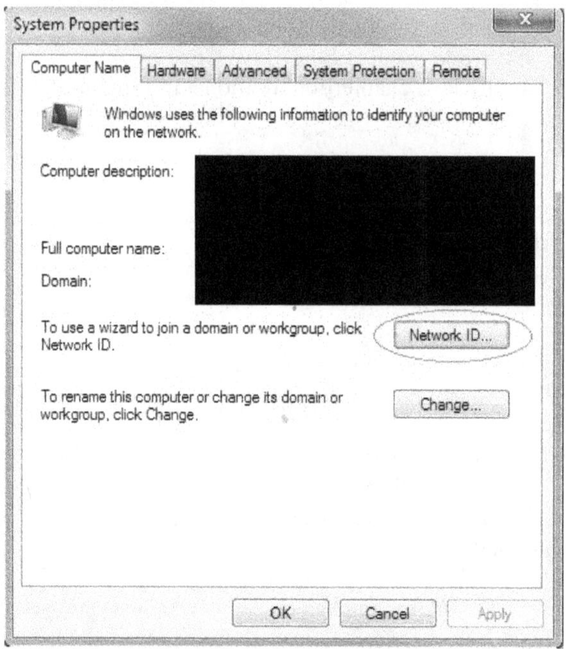

Computers, Devices, and Hardware

Computers refer to the Personal Computers, and laptops. Devices are tools used along with the computer like microphones and speakers and routers. Hardware is a more general term referring to all computer related parts like mother boards, networking objects like cables, and other related parts used generally within the computer industry.

Destination

A program or a user on a source computer connects to a destination computer in order to accomplish a task such as sending an email.

Host

Host generally refers to a Server hosting an Application or Service.

Port:

When a computer uses an Application or Service on a Server, it connects to it through a specified Port number on the Server.

Source:

See Destination.

Zone:

A zone is a group of computers networked together using similar network IP addresses and subnet masking.

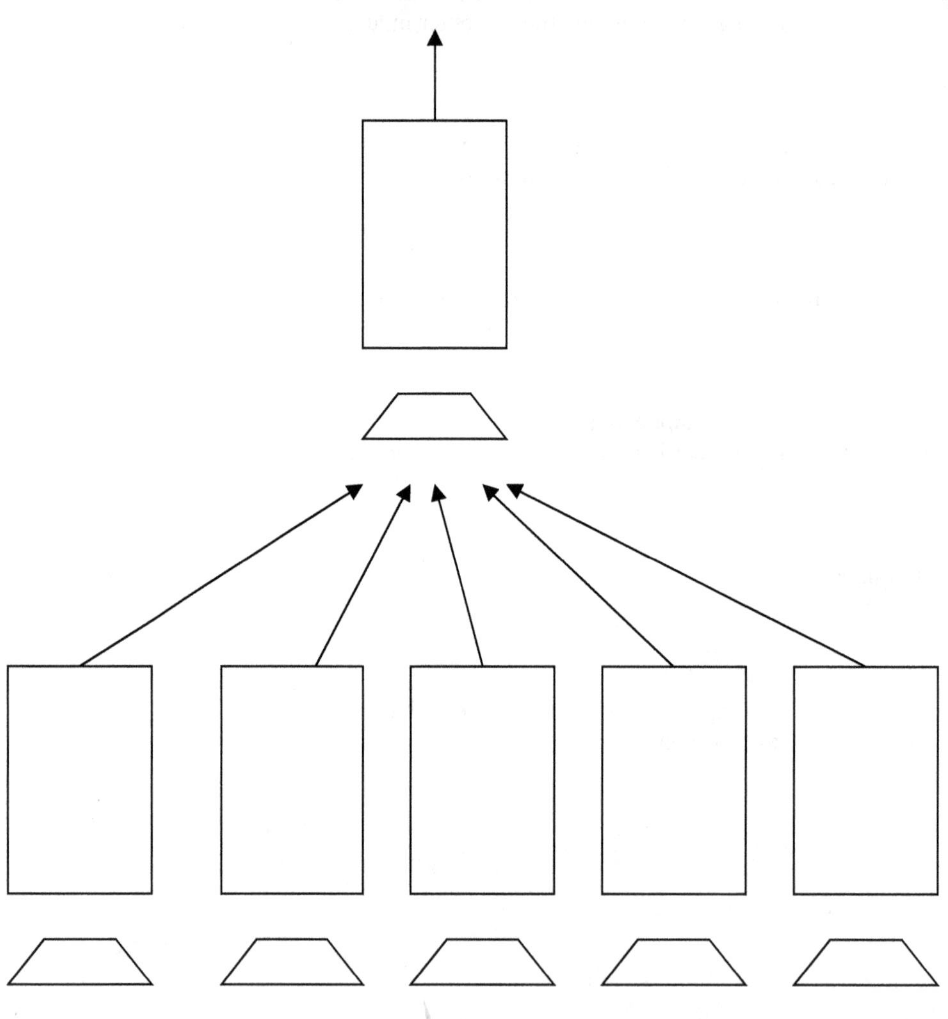

Internet

In this chapter:

1. **Internet Tools and Applications**

Internet Tools and Applications

Adobe PDF:

Adobe offers a nice tool for creating and distributing read only documents created from a Microsoft Office Application, or other document processor. Many documents on the World Wide Web are distributed in the Adobe Portable Document format. See www.adobe.com for additional details. Like a lot of tools on the Internet many Adobe tools are free. Well built freeware usually makes programmers happy unless they want to sell it. ☺

Apps:

Generally speaking Apps are Internet Hosted Applications that can be used on an Android, Cell Phone, Black Berry, Ipad, Iphone, or other mobile computer devices.

Browsers and Search Engines:

A Web Browser is used to browse the Web. The World Wide Web is the infrastructure of languages and Applications used to process and send information across a World Wide network of computers. These computers are interconnected using physical and conventional communication tools. The Browser works at the Application, Presentation and Protocol Layers of the OSI Model. See the OSI Model for more details.

Search Engines are usually Websites displayed in a Browsers that allow users to search for content on the World Wide Web. These Websites have different top level domain designators such as .com, .edu, and .gov to filter Website content down to more specific areas of interest.

The following is a list of some Browsers and Search Engines used across the Internet:

AOL: America Online provides Email, Browser, and Search Engine capabilities.

Google: Google is a company providing many Internet tools. www.google.com is the Google Search Engine.

Google Chrome: This is the Google Web Browser.

IE (Internet Explorer): This is the Microsoft Web Browser.

Microsoft Bing: This is the Microsoft Search Engine.

Mozilla Firefox: This is the Mozilla Web Browser.

Internet:

See Browser.

ISP:

EarthLink and DeltaCom are examples of Internet Service Providers. These companies will provide companies with a Router and or a Domain Controller Address that will link employees to the Internet. See Service Agreement under General Programming.

Tip:

If the ISP mentions Burst Speeds this means that they can increase the amount of data going back and forth during high moments of usage. This may refer to a software setting and it does not necessarily mean that their Fiber Optics and other Hardware is state of the art.

Root Servers:

A series of redundant World Wide Servers used to resolve Addresses across the Internet.

WWW:

World Wide Web. See Browser.

Presentation

In this chapter:

1. **Presentation Tools**

Presentation Tools

Captivate:

This tool allows presenters to take sophisticated screen shots, to show real time screen maneuvers, and to add both verbal and textual commentary to an overall project presentation. It uses a wizard tool to create the presentation which can be edited later. Coding is not necessary to perform these tasks.

Microsoft Power Point:

This tool allows presenters to create presentations. The users can add pre-created events to the presentation such as the ability to fly in or out of a page. VBA macros can be added for personalized events. There are many helpful books and websites dealing with how to use Power Point.

Microsoft Movie Maker:

Microsoft Movie Maker comes with some of the later Microsoft Operating Systems. Some versions move through the frames slower than others. Use this tool to combine pictures and sounds to make a movie. The movie saved as a MSWMM, can be easily converted to a WMV and be readily available to watch using QuickTime. Additional file converters like WinX DVD are available that will allow users to move the movie to a DVD and watch it with a DVD player. Do not forget to use a tool like the Sound Recorder utility to record some awesome sounds in order to make the movie experience more exciting!

Microsoft Paint:

Users use this tool to create or modify drawings. The tool has the ability to invert colors, add and change shapes, select coloring, add brush strokes, and make size and rotational changes. This tool is often used when creating pictures for HTML and Word documents. See Paintshop Pro for additional information. Microsoft Paint comes installed complementary with almost all Microsoft Operating Systems.

Paintshop Pro:

Paintshop Pro is an advanced tool used to create or modify drawings. The tool has the ability to invert colors, add and change shapes, select from a large selection of coloring and brush strokes, and make multiple size and rotational changes. It is used a lot of the time when creating pictures for HTML and Word documents. See Microsoft Paint for additional information.

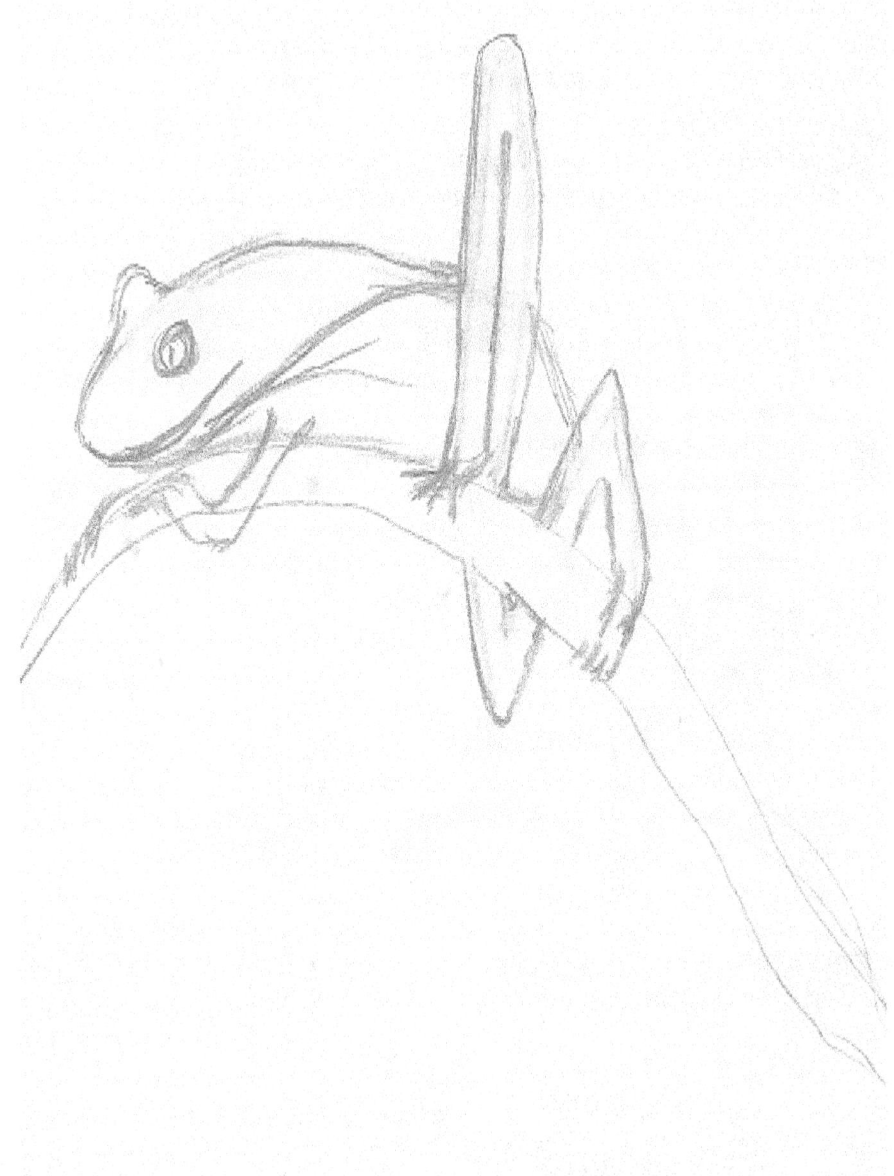

Unix And Linux

In this chapter:

1. Unix and Linux Commands

Unix and Linux servers are used a lot in business environments because they are dependable and have a variety of uses such as hosting an Oracle DB server. Users can use a putty program or a similar program to get into the server and make modifications and check property and file values. They are command line driven where as the Windows OS uses a GUI (Guided User Interface) for interaction.

Unix and Linux Commands

The following commands are used in a Unix or Linux environment to accomplish a variety of tasks. Take a look at Linux Commands in the File Types and Tools chapter for additional information.

Cat Command:

This command is used to print content from a file onto the monitor.

Example:

cat company.txt will print out the contents of the text within the company.txt file.

Cat company.txt > NewCompany.txt will create a NewCompany text file and copy the contents of the company.txt file to the new file.

Chmod Command:

Chmod changes file permissions on a linux computer. The first number sets permissions for an individual user (the owner), the second sets permissions for a group, and the third sets permissions for everyone. The numbers 0 through 7 give different permissions sets to the users. For example, 0 means the user or group has no permission, 4 means the user or group has read only permission, 6 means the user or group has read and write permissions, and 7 means the user or group has read, write, and execute permissions. It is also permissible to use a character convention such as rw in place of the number 6 with these commands.

See http://codex.wordpress.org/Changing_File_Permissions for more details about this command.

Examples: chmod 777 company.txt
chmod 123 company.txt
chmod 456 company.txt

Cron Command:

A cron job can be setup to run at specified times on a Unix or Linux Server. Cron comes from a Greek word meaning time.

Example:

This example edits the crontab file setting up a backup program to be run once a month.

```
$ crontab –e
0 0 1 * * /usr/backup/backup.exe
```

References:

1. http://www.cyberciti.biz/faq/how-do-i-add-jobs-to-cron-under-linux-or-unix-oses/
2. http://www.pantz.org/software/cron/croninfo.html

Csh and Sh Scripts:

A Corn Shell or a Shell script can be used for performing a series of commands like chmod (change mode) and cp (copy) on a Unix or Linux box. See the chmod command above.

Example:

The following hypothetical Corn Shell Script will read through some Upload* files processing data and loading it into a table. Some other examples can be found at http://www.cyberciti.biz/faq/ksh-for-loop/

```
Chmod 777 passwordFile      #file contents:  admin/admin@dbname
Variable = Cat passwordFile
Chmod 444 passwordFile
fileList="/directory/upload1 directory/upload2"
while f in $fileList; do
Echo "Processing " && fileName
Sqlldr VariableAccount fileName   # upload the file
loop
```

Rsync:

Use this tool with Linux or Unix to copy contents from a directory to directory on a remote machine. If the copy stops it will continue where it left off and ignore data that has already transferred.

rsync -avh
username@[IPAddress]:/[DirectoryPath]/[Filename.Extension] .
or
rsync -avh username@[IPAddress]:/[DirectoryPath] .

Secure Copy SCP:

Secure Copy is a Linux or Unix tool used to encrypt a file or group of files and transfer it/them from or to a Source or Destination computer.

Tar:

Tar is used to compress files. The files can be untarred later. This is similar to the winzip tool used with Windows files. English professors everywhere love it when computer people talk about untarring files. ☺

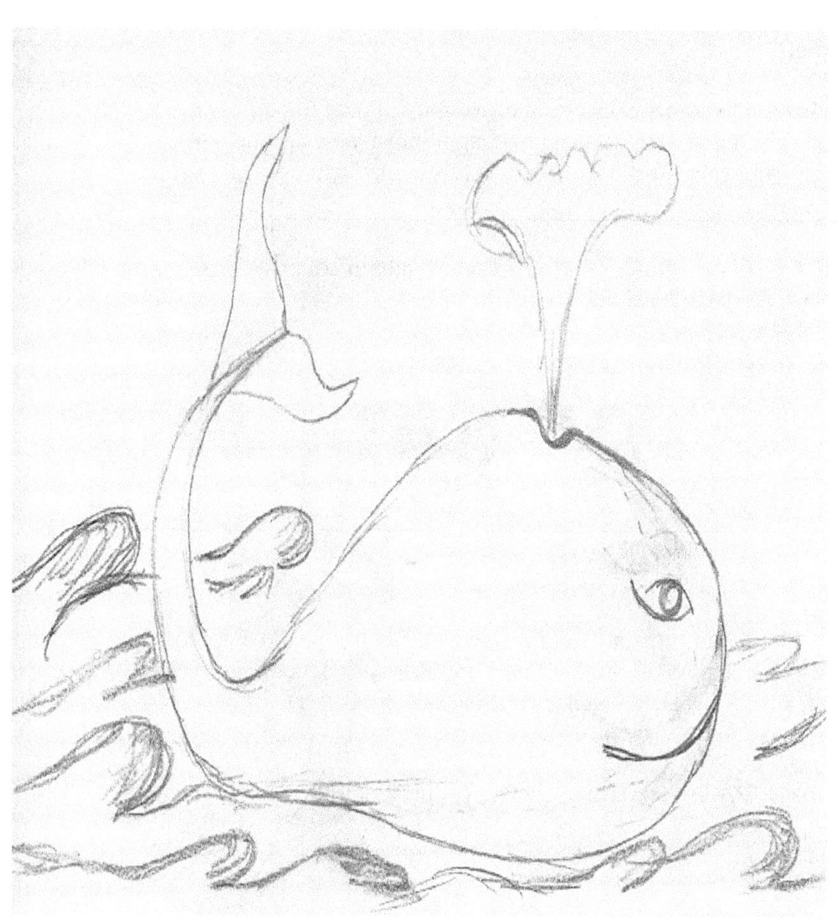

Java

In this chapter:

1. **Object Oriented Terminology**
2. **Java Tools**
3. **Java Objects and Applications**
4. **Programming in Java**
5. **Java Errors Occurring Frequently**

Object Oriented Terminology

Java is a powerful modern language that works off of object oriented classes. A parent class is used to define characteristics and methods for a child or various children classes. The following terms will help to further solidify the concepts behind object oriented programming.

Abstract Class:

See Class. This is basically a template – a cookie cutter class is used to create other classes.

Tip:

Take a look at Learning Java by O'Reilly Media and other Java books for additional information. Also look at the http://www.tutorialspoint.com/java/ website which is a great reference for learning about Java and many other programming languages.

Class:

The class descriptor is used a lot with .NET and Java programming. There are different kinds of classes and they inherit characteristics and abilities from other classes. For example a developer can create a parent food class with attributes such as color, taste, and smell, and then further define what food is by creating sub classes like dairy, vegetables, and meat. Each subclass may have additional properties and methods. Classes can also be used to delegate tasks and instantiate tasks using other classes at their disposal as permitted by the code.

Encapsulation:

Encapsulation occurs when variables inside a class, method, or another object, take on parameter values passed to an object. When this occurs the scope and the assingment of these variable values become dependant upon or encapsulated within the new object accepting these parameters.

Inheritance:

Inheritance occurs when one class object Inherits properties and methods from another class. For instance the Lamborghini class may inherit properties from a parent car class.

Interface:

This is a piece of code that relegates what and how methods are used within a specific class object. Note that the delegate command is used to instantiate the interface before the methods are called.

Instantiation:

Instantiation occurs when a developer creates or assigns an instance of a class or an interface.

Overloading:

Overloading occurs when a method is defined multiple times so that can accept more than one set of parameters. For instance a CreateBank Account method could be created with a member name and social security number or with a phone number and a member ID.

Polymorphism:

This refers to the ability of a class method to take on multiple capabilities depending on specific situations. See Overloading.

Java Tools

AJAX:

AJAX objects are configurable tools or components used with .NET and Java based applications to enrich the functionality of an application. For instance a developer may incorporate an AJAX calendar to see dates and times in new and exciting ways. Be careful. The cost of the AJAX toolsets can add up if a company is on a tight budget and still in the design phase of a project.

ANT:

This tool is used to package a group of Java files into a WAR file. It can also be used to deploy WAR files to the server. See WAR file.

Tip:

WAR file deployment can also be accomplished through other tools like the Oracle Enterprise Manager.

AspectJ:

AspectJ works along with Java IDEs such as Eclipse to add aspects to Java code. An Aspect is like a DB trigger. The aspect functionality fires when a Java method fires cutting in and performing another task instead of or before or after a method is run. Java.NET has the aspect ability to "cut in" (or make a cut) when an application is performing a task as well.

Eclipse:

This free IDE allows developers to create software using the Java language. It integrates well with the file system and offers some nice development features like intellisense typing and coding examples. It can be used to develop several application types used on the client, across a network, or on the Internet.

Flash:

This software platform can be used to create plugins that are not Java based. Flas allows developers to add visual affects to a website like moving borders and morphing backgrounds. Flash is used to give websites and mobile devices a sense of flare and excitement.

JavaBeans:

JavaBeans are Java components that are reusable. JavaBeans can provide information to an application such as session IDs, account information, and the host name of a computer being used. They can also be used to provide functionality such as user alerts as well as sound and display prompts. JavaBeans consist of Java classes and encapsulate objects within a single bean container that can be configured internally and passed around between different technology and different modules. AppletInitializer, Customizer, and PropertyEditor are examples of Interfaces used by JavaBeans. Certain rules must be followed in order to meet the conventions layed out when developing JavaBean classes. For instance, JavaBean classes should be serializable. These beans are developed by many different IDEs such as Oracle JDeveloper and used in many modern applications. Adding a bean to an Oracle Form, for example, is as simple as dragging the bean from a library and dropping it into the form. [1]

Reference:
1. Thomas Candina, Senior Application Developer, 31-Jan-2012, ATS Email Communication

Java Objects and Applications

Applet:

This is a Java program that runs in its own container over a web browser. An Applet offers a wide variety of functionality such as the ability to access and modify data within a DB table.

Case Study 1:

"Hello World" is a simple Applet that displays a message within a Java based applet on a web browser.

Reference:
Mary Campione and Kathy Walrath, The Java Tutorial Object-Oriented Programming for the Internet, Sun Microsystems, Inc, 1996p. 13

The walkthrough at https://www.science.uva.nl/ict/ossdocs/java/tutorial/getStarted/applet/index.html provides step by step instructions for running the "Hello World" applet in a browser.

Components:

When one Java program can be used with another to perform related tasks these programs are known as components. For instance, one component may be used to login to an application and another component may be used to select DB payroll information.

Javascript:

Javascript is a scripting language used with Internet web pages. It can be included inside the HTML page or as a linked file. It relies heavily on the Java language and is able to modify and interact with website items.

Java Server Faces:

Java Server Faces split Java development up into objects drawing from architectural theory known as the Model View Controller.
This splits the application into three categories focusing on 1) loging in and usingdata, 2) interfacing with the user, and 3). Application processing. The tutorial at http://www.tutorialspoint.com/jsf/ describes this architecture and gives a good overview of this powerful language.

JDeveloper

JDeveloper allows developers to create software using the Java language. It integrates well with the file system and offers some nice development features like intellisense typing and readily available coding examples. It can be used to develop several application types used either on the client, across a network, or on the Internet.

Jquery:

Jquery is the Java Script library used to assist with client side scripting.

JSON:

JSON is a language agnostic data interchange standard. That mean it works with many different languages. Java Script Object Notation is used with Java Script, as well as other languages, to serialize and deserialize data as it is passed back and forth between various coding pieces. A good example of when this is used would be when recursively processing a cookie or file to cycle through a shopping list. REST and JSON are becoming the preferred methods over SOAP for passing data back and forth between applications.

Reference:
http://www.bamboorocketapps.com/rest-json-vs-soap-xml/

JUNIT:

This tool is used to test Java applications more effectively. The developer creates a test to verify that each piece of the Java program is working. JUNIT runs all of these tests returning their results to a web page that the developer team can review on a predetermined time sensitive basis.

Microsoft Silverlight:

Microsoft Sliverlight is a Java alternative tool used to produce website plugins. The plugins are used to give mobile devices a sense of flare and excitement. It is being used frequently in many modern SharePoint Applications. See SharePoint under File Types and Tools.

Mobile Java Server Faces:

See Server Faces. This modification to JSF allows the JSF architecture and syntax to be applied to a mobile application or device. See http://mobiforge.com/book/mobile-jsf for additional information.

Netbeans:

Netbeans is a free IDE that allows developers to create software using the Java language. It integrates well with the file system and offers some nice development features like intelisense typing and coding examples. It can be used to develop several application types used on the client, across a network, or on the Internet.

Prime Faces:

Prime Faces is a user interface library used with Java Server Faces.

Rich Faces:

Rich Faces is a user interface library used with Java Server Faces.

Spring:

The Spring language is a language framework that has become popular among Java Developers. It includes many nice capabilities like cross cutting, messaging, and transaction control. Take a look at http://en.wikipedia.org/wiki/Spring_Framework for additional information.

Singleton Session Bean:

A singleton bean is specific to the application and is instantiated when the application lifecycle begins. Beans are used when developing Java applications using specifications like Java Server Faces. See http://docs.oracle.com/javaee/6/tutorial/doc/gipjg.html for additional information.

Statefull Session Bean:

If a JavaBean is statefull it means that the value in the JavaBean is client specific. Beans are used when developing Java applications using specifications like Java Server Faces. See http://docs.oracle.com/javaee/6/tutorial/doc/gipjg.html for additional information.

Stateless Session Bean:

If a JavaBean is stateless this means that the value in the Bean is not client specific. Beans are used when developing Java applications using specifications like Java Server Faces. See http://docs.oracle.com/javaee/6/tutorial/doc/gipjg.html for additional information.

WAR:

A Web Archive File is used to provide information for deploying a set of Java files used in an application.

Programming In Java

In short there are a few IDEs available for Programming in Java including Eclipse and JDeveloper. Java is a powerful Object Oriented Language with a powerful set of functions used for dealing with drawings, integers, strings, and other objects. This language is powerful and accomplishes tasks quickly. The only downside is that the community has created so many IDEs, functions, and Java versions it is sometimes difficult to determine the best way to move forward.

Here are a few commands or conventions used with the Java language:

&& Used when comparing values with conditional logic, && is used in place of AND.
|| Used when comparing values with conditional logic, || is used in place of OR.
Alert Used to alert the user with a message.
Integer.toString(variable) Converts a variable to a String.
Str.lower Converts a String to a lower case String.
Str.match Checks to see if one String equals another.
Str.replace Replaces a String value with another value.
Str.slice Extract part of a String into another String.
Str.split Splits record values based on a delimeter.
Str.substring Looks for a Substring within a String.

Str.upper Converts a String to upper case.
String.parseInt (variable) Parses a String as an Integer value.

Java works well for reading a document and manipulating strings. The following commands are used to create a buffered reader that can be used to analyze individual words on a website.

```
URL urlVariable = new URL(http://www.mywebsite/);
BReader in = newBufferedReader(new
InputStreamReader(urlVariable.openStream()));

//A loop and a String reader would also be needed to accomplish this.
```

Developers can read more about how to achieve this requirement at the following URL:
http://docs.oracle.com/javase/tutorial/networking/urls/readingURL.html

Case Study 1:

Opening a secure socket example:

Time Servers around the world are used to provide the correct time for domain servers and other devices in different locations. A secure socket layer adds data to packets passed back and forth on the internet. This data is used to ensure only the correct users have service access. Use the code from these websites to see and possibly program a service that a developer might use with SSL to read write the time from a time server service provider:

1. http://stackoverflow.com/questions/385907/java-client-to-connect-to-server-with-openssl-and-client-auth/
2. http://stackoverflow.com/questions/7081262/getting-time-from-public-time-server-using-timetcpclient
3. http://www.informit.com/articles/article.aspx?p=26316&seqNum=3
4. http://www.javawebdevelop.com/2717185/

Case Study 2:

The Knapsack Problem occurs when a developer desires to determine the best way to distribute a certain amount of items with specified sizes in the least amount of containers as possible. The Greedy Algorithm can be used to resolve "the Knapsack Problem". See the example graph below. A program might be given several knapsacks and asked to fill the knapsack with varying size objects.

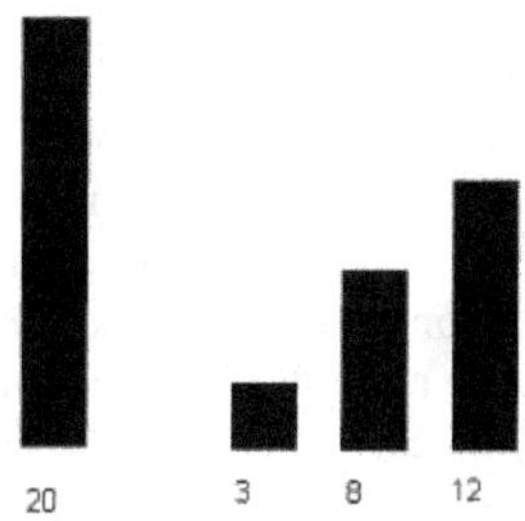

K >	0	1	2	3	4	5	6	7	8	9	10	11	12	13	14	15	16	17	18	19	20
i1=3	0	-	-	Y_a	-	-	-	-	-	-	-	-	-	-	-	-	-	-	-	-	-
i2=8	0	-	-	0	-	-	-	-	Y_b	-	-	Y_c	-	-	-	-	-	-	-	-	-
i3=12	0	-	-	0	-	-	-	-	0	-	-	0	Y_d	-	-	Y_e	-	-	-	-	Y_f

- Means a solution does not exist yet
0 Means that a solution has already been found
Y_a Says that item 1 goes into 3 filling the knapsack(k=3).
Y_b Says that item 2 goes into 8 filling the knapsack(k=8).
Y_c Says that items 1 and 2 go into 8 filling the knapsack(k=11).
Y_d Says that item 3 goes into 12 filling the knapsack(k=12).
Y_e Says that items 1 and 3 go into 15 filling the knapsack(k=15).
Y_f Says that items 2 and 3 go into 20 filling the knapsack(k=20).

References:

1. Introduction To Algorithms, 2nd Edition, The Massachusetts Institute of Technology, 2001 p. 382

See https://www.youtube.com/watch?v=cEqCdRzWLCY for a tutorial that shows how to use Java to solve a knapsack problem.

Case Study 3:

Check out the following website to see how Dr. Mike creates a networked tic tac toe program using Java. This includes information for how to create a (GUI) Guided User Interface for multiple users.

www.dr-mikes-maths.com/tictactoe.html

Java Errors Occurring Frequently:

A few general functionality notes: Ensure that the Windows Classpath is setup under Computer Properties - Advanced - Environmental Properties. Java IDEs are constanty changing, so developers may need to upgrade to a newer (or an older) version of an IDE to get the functionality to work. When distributing an Oracle application try to ensure that all of the clients are using the correct Oracle version of Java etc. Also note that some client machines, monitors, or devices may work differently with different software.

Reference:
Tyler Gates, Senior Applications Developer, 18-Jun-2014, ATS Email Communication

Tip:

When using Eclipse, ensure that the classpath is setup under Computer Properties - Advanced - Environmental Properties.

Code has been deprecated:

Java is constantly updating the way their functions work. If a developer encounters this error he or she should look for the replacement code that performs the task that needs to be completed. For instance, it may be necessary to stop using a function like the DataInputStreams and use the BufferedReader function instead.

Reference:
http://stackoverflow.com/questions/18961673/java-deprecation-readline-in-datainputstream-has-been-deprecated

Connection Issues:
Verify that the Database or Server is running.

Error 1714. The older version of Java cannot be removed.

This occurs if the registry keys have been damaged. Use the Microsoft Fix it utility to correct this.

General java related errors:

See http://cs-people.bu.edu/dgs/courses/cs111/assignments/errors.html for a list of common errors and how to handle them.

Import.java.util does not exist:

Install a newer version of Java and see if it corrects the problem.

Persistence:

If a developer sees errors that say things like Persistence unit not found or No persistence.xml file found in project, he or she may need to recreate the Java folder structure as described at

http://stackoverflow.com/questions/17695458/eclipse-how-to-fix-error-no-persistence-xml-file-found-in-project-jpa-issue
and https://community.jboss.org/message/735385

General Programming

In this chapter:

1. General Terms and Tools

General Terms and Tools

The following is a list of some important terms a developer might encounter when programming or working on a project.

Access Control List:

The Access Control List governs who has rights to do what with various objects in a file system.

Activity Diagram:

An Activity Diagram includes several columns. The columns represent areas of work performed by a computer application. Pictures and arrows within and between the columns describe the desired tasks that the software should perform for specified user(s) at various times.

Action Request System:

This is a ticketing system, like Remedy or Ticket Tracker used to create workflow objects that can be used with a wide variety of projects.

Agile Programming:

The Agile Programming methodology is a technique that some Software development groups use to design Software. Using this technique, a high level software design occurs and an initial prototype is developed, unit tested, and tested by the customer representative. Use Case Scenarios, Activity Diagrams, and State Charts are used to further develop and communicate the design to the developer and the user group. After the initial product is developed, a customer representative gives feedback and the process begins again until a more permanent solution develops. Read through the Agile For Dummies book, compliments of IBM, to learn more about this subject.

One additional observation: It is important to communicate with your boss and co-workers. If a person prefers to ask questions over Instant Message or Email, instead of face to face, that will probably work, but stay in touch.

Reference:
http://en.wikipedia.org/wiki/Agile_software_development

Air Traffic Control:

An ATC has to keep up with many details about planes, weather, and objects on the ground. It needs to be able to warn pilots as soon as possible if there is a conflict or an unexpected turn of events. Collision Avoidance Systems must be programmed with a high level of attention to detail to ensure the safety of the crew, other people, and objects on the ground and in the air.

Reference:
en.wikipedia.org/wiki/Air_traffic_control

Artificial Intelligence:

Artificial Intelligence refers to programming a computer so that it can learn and then use that knowledge in the future. An example of incorporating Artificial Intelligence in an application would be the new IBM Watson computer that was recently tested on Jeopardy! IBM trained it well enough to beat the human competition. Prolog and Lisp are examples of Artificial Intelligence programming languages.

Assembly Language:

Assembly Language works very intimately with the machine level language. If the language that runs the inner workings of the computer has a command to add variables the Assembly Language will have a corresponding command that mirrors it. See Binary Code.

Binary Code:

This language provides a one to one bit mapping of the machine level language commands. Zeros and ones are used to represent these commands or various machine commands. Some machine level command examples include Add, Load, and Store.
The binary values below represent the numbers 1, 2, and 5 in binary. The 1 at the far right is 1^0, the 1 beside that is 1^1, and the 1 in the third position from the right represents 1^2. The machine adds these numbers together to represent 0 through 255. See Assembly Language for more information.

00000001 = 1
00000010 = 2
00000101 = 5

Boiler Plate Objects:

These are not hot plates. Boiler Plate Objects are lines, graphics, texts, or other reusable objects located in a module like an Oracle Form.

Borland Software Corporation:

Borland Software Corporation provides tools used primarily to facilitate and to develop Software projects. Some products include Borland Caliber and Borland StarTeam. The reader can learn more about Borland products at http://www.borland.com/products.

Borland Caliber:

This tool is used during the process of developing a piece of software. It allows analyst to enter all of the software requirements as they pertain to a project or a sub-project. After the initial information is entered the analysts and developers can track their tasks to see what has and what has not been completed. Security and advanced reporting features are also available.

Borland Starteam:

Borland Starteam is an integrated tool used along with software files for change management and project management.

Branching:

Branching occurs when a piece of code takes two or more different paths. For instance, one version may remain the same and the other version may incorporate changes specific to a subset of companies.

CAD:

These Computer Aided Dispatch tools are used to dispatch personnel to a point of interest and track their progress as an event unfolds.

Case:

A case statement accepts an expression and does different things with that expression depending on the condition or the result. A Case statement can be used within a select statement as well.
Here are a few examples of what an Oracle based case statement might look like:

```
 --From Oracle Forms
CASE vTeamSize
      WHEN 1 THEN call_alert('success','The value is 1.');
      WHEN 2 THEN call_alert('success','The value is 2.');
            ELSE call_alert('success','The value is 3 or more.');
      END;

 --From an Oracle Database
 SELECT salary,
            CASE
      WHEN date_column_name IS NULL THEN '1-JAN-1900'
      WHEN TRUNC(date_column_name) = SYSDATE THEN
      'Today'
       ELSE 'Other'
       END return_date FROM dual;
```

Certificates:

There are various kinds of Certificates. A Public key is used to encrypt data and send it to another specified user who is the only person that can decrypt it with his or her Private key certificate.

See http://www.smallbusinessnewz.com/top-five-ssl-certificate-providers-2008-03 for more information regarding SSL Certificates and Certificate Providers. Here is a list of popular Certificate Providers:

Comodo
GoDady
Verisign

Reference:
David L. Prowse, CompTIA Security + SY0-301 Authorized Cert Guide, Pearson Education, Inc, 2012 page 421

Class:

See Class under the Java chapter.

ClickYes Pro 2010:

Microsoft Outlook has security alerts that require a user to verify if he or she wants to do tasks like send emails. This Software can be called from a program and is used to automatically accept these security warnings.

Client:

A client a computer that relies on a server or set of servers on a network to provide networking information and other information the client may need when an operator runs an application.

Cloud Technology:

One example of cloud technology would be modern day gaming technology like Wii Sports. Another example would be Google Docs. The provider does not specify to the connected users where the technology is stored or how it works. It may be stored on one or more servers using multiple operating systems and multiple programming languages.

www.Rackspace.com is an example of a cloud provider providing various computer technology and back end services. Users log in and access their data with little knowledge of what is occurring on the back end.

www.Office360.com is an example of a Microsoft Cloud service. This service allows companies to utilize multiple operating systems, applications, and backup technology. For instance, a user can choose to use Microsoft Outlook and Microsoft Share Point on a Windows 7 Professional Box and he or she can expect Office 360 to backup the data stored there for company users as part of the service agreement.

Code Review:

Important Note: If a developer is not sure about something in his or her code, regardless of the size of the code or script, it is important to have another developer or manager review the code to ensure it is correct. This will protect the developer from implementing a fix that could be detrimental to his or her career. See Unit Test and Quality Test.

Comments:

Comments are descriptive wording used in code to explain what the code is doing, who coded it, and when it was coded.

Command Prompt:

This is a computer prompt that accepts commands from the user and provides output.

Console App:

A console app is an application that accepts text commands from the user. It is commonly used to perform tasks such as going through a payroll Database and calculating end of month calculations.

Continue:

The continue statement is generally used to ignore a code piece within a loop and to move on to the next iteration of the loop.

Control:

Controls are Development Environment objects like text and image items that are used in an application.

Cookies:

Cookies are files stored on a client used to track browser history and other information that relate to how a user uses an Internet Application.

Copy and Paste:

Users can use keyboard shortcuts like Ctrl + c and Ctrl + v to copy selected text information from one place and paste it somewhere else.

Cowboy Programming:

This means someone is basically programming by the seat of their pants with few safety checks in place such as code reviews and tests.

Connection String:

A string used in .NET applications and other applications to connect to a system, a DB, or a Web Service.

Content Management System:

A CMS allows employees to store files in a secure way with company hierarchies and permissions. Magento and Livelink are examples of Content Management Systems.

Crystal Reports:

This is an Adhoc tool incorporating data connections and queries, grid items and controls, and parameters to pull data from a Database or other area and present it to the user in a very effective way.

Data Types:

A Type used to define a variable or a table field. Some data types include varchars, numbers, chars, booleans, and dates.

Data Warehouse:

This is a data location where large amounts of data are consolidated from various locations like databases and emails and then used for analysis and reporting. See http://en.wikipedia.org/wiki/Data_warehouse for more information.

DCL:

Digital Command Language. This programming language is used in old vax systems to create applications. The author used it at one point to modify a program used to search through warehouse items and return quantity and location information.

Debugging:

Debugging occurs when a programmer inserts pauses and messages within code and watches the variable values to study problem areas. It is very useful when someone is able to do this successfully because it prevents a great amount of frustration on the user end. On the DB side developers should learn to create a "debug" table with a large enough column or columns to track what is happening when a problem occurs. Developers may need to insert debug data from objects like functions, procedures, and triggers in order to allow them to know where a glitch occurs and what process led to the problem. This technique can be used on the application side as well, but it may be better to use alerts or messages there. Developers should try to capture information right before the error occurs and then work further out if necessary.

Decryption:

Mathematics can be used to encrypt strings and numbers so that no one else is able to read the values until they are decrypted. Similar mathematical techniques can be used to make the file readable or decrypted. See Encryption below

Design Document:

This document is used to describe project design details to a developer. A coding standards document can be used as well to define conventions for coding specific features such as list items and push buttons.

Distributed System Solution:

In a distributed system various OS and application combinations work together to solve a problem. Cloud computing may use a similar technique, but everything is done under the covers on a computer or many computers somewhere on the network or over the Internet.

DOS:

The Disk Operating System is a system developed by IBM that uses a command line interface and can work with attached input devices.

eBlvd:

This is a cloud based technology like Pcanywhere that lets a user attach to one or multiple computers to manage and or support them remotely.

Encryption:

See Decryption.

Enterprise Business Suite:

This tool is used to host Oracle Applications and other functionality at the Enterprise level.

Exit:

The exit statement is generally used to exit a piece of code like a function or procedure. It could be used as the very first command if the developer does not want to run into any glitches. ☺

Findstr:

This is a special command used to find text within files in MS Dos.

findstr /c:"create table" *.sql > a.txt

TextPad
[0,2,4]* regexpressions MARK Subdirectories
[^\n\r]*
https://stackoverflow.com/questions/18858334/how-can-i-use-regular-expressions-in-textpad-to-remove-anything-line-by-line-a

Rsync
rsync -avhn --progress --partial
iasuser@XX.X.XXX.XXX:/opt/oraapps/middleware/OHPFRD/forms/atsopenone/source/client/ .

Fortran:

Fortran has been around for a while. It is case sensitive and position sensitive. It is most powerful when computing large quantities of data and results because it does not have a huge amount overhead such as large function libraries. It was originally developed by IBM to work in this manner.

Reference:
http://en.wikibooks.org/wiki/Fortran/Hello_world

Example:

The following fortran code is a modification of the example found at http://en.wikibooks.org/wiki/Fortran/Hello_world. It prints the word Greetings.

Name: greetings.f

Program:

```
program greetings

  print *, "Greetings"

end program greetings


! Command to perform compilation:  g95 greetings.f
```

Function:

A function performs a specific task for another code piece, like sorting a table or adding some numbers. It can return a value like a procedure, but does not have to.

Example:

This pl/sql example accepts a table and an order type and will return a table like a grocery list after sorting the records in a specified way.

```
FUNCTION RandomListSort (pRandomListTab IN RandomListTab,
                                    pOrderType        IN VARCHAR2)
  RETURN RandomListTab IS

    vRandomListTab     RandomListTab   := pRandomListTab
    vOrderTest             VARCHAR2(4)       := pOrderType;
    vTempRandomListTab  RandomListTab;
    vString           VARCHAR2(512);

  BEGIN

   IF vRandomListTab.COUNT > 0 THEN
    FOR i IN vRandomListTab.FIRST .. vRandomListTab.LAST
    LOOP
```

```
      vTempRandomListTab(i) := vRandomListTab(i);
    END LOOP;
    FOR i IN vTempRandomListTab.FIRST + 1 ..
      vTempRandomListTab.LAST LOOP
      vString := vTempRandomListTab(i);
      FOR j IN REVERSE vTempRandomListTab.FIRST.. (i-1)
      LOOP
        IF vTempRandomListTab(j) >= vString  THEN
          vTempRandomListTab(j+1) := vTempRandomListTab(j);
          vTempRandomListTab(j)   := vString;
        END IF;
      END LOOP;
    END LOOP;
  END IF;

  IF vOrderTest = 'ASC' THEN
    RETURN vTempRandomListTab;

ELSIF vOrderTest = 'DESC' THEN
    RETURN RandomListSort_Desc(vTempRandomListTab);
  END IF;
 END RandomListSort;
```

Fuzzy Logic:

If one apple is 200 grams and another apple is 230 grams then does one apple really equal one apple? If one person is born at the beginning of the year and the other person is born at the end of the year with different age related traits are these people really the same age? These are examples of fuzzy logic. A computer program can be built to handle questions like these, but there are a lot of variables involved. See Wikipedia for additional information.

Garbage Collection:

Some programs are able to deallocate related cursors and other structures after use. For instance, in .NET the Using statement can be incorporated for this purpose.

Get

This designation is quite often used at the beginning of a function or procedure to get data from somewhere else and store it somewhere that is easily accessed from the calling program. Developers will see this designation often in .Net, Java, and Oracle code et cetera. See the Set command later in this chapter.

Glassdoor.com

Use the glassdoor website to compare the various work ethics and benefit related aspects of one company with another. This website is also useful to developers who want to compare the salaries of various computer language related positions.

Global Variables:

A global variable is a variable that can be used throughout an application. For instance, a global variable could be a name referenced in the DB, and on various forms and reports.

Global Temporary Table:

A global temporary table can be created in Oracle to pull temp data and display it somewhere like in a form or on a report. It is a good idea to delete data from these tables after using them unless the configuration is set to do this automatically. See Allocation.

Google Docs:

Google Docs provides real time access and modification of Internet shared Google documents and Spreadsheets.

Google Glass:

Google Glasses, AKA Google Glass, has designed a pair of glasses that users can wear to interact with a variety of tool created by a variety of companies. These tools feature facial recognition, sketching abilities and translation to name a few. Glass developers use an Application Programming Interface called Mirror API to develop software for the glasses. One very exciting aspect of Google Glass is that it allows someone else to see what another person is seeing and doing and provide expert advice. In other words a programmer in one country could walk another programmer in another country through some complicated code modifications and then assist with any additional debugging and coding necessary to complete the application. This may also has relevance in the future to other fields such as Medicine, Public Safety, and Electronics. Find out more at http://en.wikipedia.org/wiki/Google_glasses.

Google Plus:

This Website features many social services such as document collaboration and personalized web pages.

Google Translate:

The website at http://translate.google.com can take a group of words or even a document and translate it from one language to another. A Microsoft Word document can do the same thing. See Microsoft Word.

Google Maps:

Developers can integrate this tool with their Internet application to provide mapping details of a location of interest. Google maps is located at https://maps.google.com. This website tool also allows users to hewn in on an area and see pictures from an unspecified time.

GoTo:

In some languages like VBA, a GoTo statement can be used to move the processing code to a specified line. The use of GoTo is not recommended because it can yield unpredictable results. If a developer wants to move outside of a programming block like an Oracle For or While Loop, it is better to use an Exit or a Continue statement.

Hexadecimal:

This is a numeric positioning of numbers that features a base of sixteen. See Binary above.

Host:

A Host is a Server hosting programs and services for client computers.

IDE:

This is an Integrated Development Environment. These tools are used to integrate a development application with a file system and can sometimes communicate with a software versioning system like PVCS or Subversion as well. See Eclipse, .NET, Oracle JDeveloper etc.

Tip:

Whether developing or querying or checking email it is always helpful to minimize the amount of windows a user has open and to keep things organized. For instance, when using the PL/SQL Developer or Toad try to put all of the selections in one SQL Window instead of several windows. Be sure to arrange OS and Email directories to allow for easy searches and retrievals.

Image:

An image is a picture used in a document or Application.

Important Names:

Bill Gates: The founder of Microsoft.
Dennis Richie: Helped to invent UNIX.
Kenneth Thompson: Helped to invent UNIX.
Larry Elison: The founder of Oracle.
Linus Torvalds: The inventor of the LINUX OS.
Steve Jobs: The founder of Apple.
Et cetera: This list could take up another book. ☺

Index:

An index can be added to a file system or Database table so the underlying query engines will know how to sort the data when selecting from and inserting data into an object. There is an example of creating a unique index under the MySQL subsection under the Databases section of this book.

Intellisense:

This type ahead functionality will determine the most likely choices for what the user is going to type and give him or her the option to select from those choices. For example, if a developer types select * from employee where… the IDE may provide a drop down with several fields to choose from ranging from the employee name to the employee salary or department.

InStr:

InStr is a function used to determine where a value occurs in a string.

Iterate:

To iterate means to move to the next item in a set of objects.

IVR:

This stands for Interactive Voice Response System. It essentially incorporates computer programming with a voice response system.

Keyboard Shortcuts:

Programmers use keyboard shortcuts to perform tasks more easily. For instance a user can save a Word Document by clicking ctrl + s inside the document. Here are some additional Windows OS shortcuts:

ctrl + c = copy
ctrl + v = paste
ctrl + a = select all
ctrl + shift + tab = choose applications in 2D
ctrl + [windows button] + tab = choose applications in 3D
ctrl + shift + n = incognito browsing
ctrl + shift + t = search last browsed website
ctrl + shift + c = to see browser elements
ctrl + w = close an open object like a document.

ctrl + y = redo an action
ctrl + z = undo an action
[windows button] + left or right arrow = moves minimized window to different locations.

Reference:
http://windows.microsoft.com/en-us/windows/keyboard-shortcuts#keyboard-shortcuts=windows-7

License:

A license gives a user permission to run a program or IDE under specified conditions. Some licenses permit a user to use a program for free. Others may require a slightly larger payment. ☺

Lists:

Lists could refer to various things like a small SharePoint lookup record group or to a large list box for selecting values in an Oracle Form.

Locks:

See Locks under Database Technology.

Mapquest:

Use the Mapquest tool at www.mapquest.com to get driving locations from one point to another. This tool looks somewhat like a GPS, but it does not know the user's location unless he or she provides it.

Microsoft Project:

This application allows a manager or team leader to track who is on a project, when deliverables are due, and whether or not the deliverables are being met on time.

Mod:

Mod is a common programming function. It is used to determine the remainder of the result after dividing two numbers. For example, if 5 goes into 12 two times this function will return a remainder of 2.

Performance:

Performance relates to the overall efficiency of a program. It incorporates speed, efficiency, and other cost variables to determine how code compares with other code. See Index for more details.

Perl:

Perl a scripting language used to pull and manipulate data associated with an Operating System or Server Database. Take a look at http://www.perl.com/pub/2000/10/begperl1.html for a comprehensive Perl tutorial.

Pointer:

The pointer concept is used in C and other languages with objects types like the array to point to a specified place in memory that holds a value for the object containing the data.

Office 365:

This is a cloud related service that allows a company to utilize Microsoft servers, and to hosts MS Office products like a SharePoint Portal.

Operator Precedence:

Programming operators have an order by which they run. For instance in most languages the following calculation: 9 + 3 / 4 x 5 will multiply 4 times 5 and then divide 3 by 20 and then add 9. If a parenthesis is added as shown here: (9 + 3) / (4 x 5) the calculation will add 9 + 3 as the numerator before dividing it by the denominator of 20. So this would equal .6 without the parenthesis and 12.75 with the parenthesis.

Operating System (OS):

This is the software system or systems used to run and coordinate all of the other software programs for a computer. For instance Windows works on top of DOS using core Visual Basic scripts. Programs like

MS Word, PL SQL Developer, and XML Spy are developed to work on top of the VBA scripted environment once the OS has booted up. Take a look at some of the various books for Dos, Linux, Mac, and Windows to find out more about Operating Systems.

OSI Model:

Various layers should be considered when working with a computer application. At the Physical Layer cat 5 cables and wireless routers etc. move 0s and 1s back and forth within the data layer. At the Network Layer, the Transmission Control Protocol / Internet Protocol, the Simple Mail Transport Protocol, and many other protocols are used to connect and process the data. Then, at the Data Layer, the Application layer, and the Presentation layer data is processed and presented to the users in a variety of ways. This model is very similar to the holistic approach of medicine. We all have a mental, spiritual, emotional, and physical side. It is almost as important to present ourselves in a professional way as it is to build up our mental capabilities by reading books like these. However, emotional stability is also important. ☺

OTR:

This stands for Off The Record. It is a tool used to encrypt instant messaging using Pidgin with a higher level of privacy. See Pidgin under General Programming.

Package:

A package is an Oracle object. It consists of a Package Specification and a Package Body file. The specification is sometimes just referred to as the specification file. Developers will generally include function and procedure headers or definitions in the specification file. The header along with the actual module will be in the package body file. If developers only include functions and procedure headers in the package body they will be hidden to everyone that is not accessing a public object within the body. See the Reference Cursor section under the Oracle chapter for an example.

Pcanywhere:

This tool allows a user to connect to a client machine, see what the client users see, and make updates to the client. See Remote Desktop as well.

Pidgin:

Pidgin is a free Instant Messaging tool that allows users to send messages and small icons back and forth on the Network. An OTR Plugin is used to encrypt the messages. To use Pidgin download and install the Application found at https://www.pidgin.im/download. To use the OTR tool download and install the exe from https://otr.cypherpunks.ca, then go to tools – plugins, and activate the OTR plugin and generate An encryption key. See OTR under the Security chapter.

Procedure:

This is a program that generally accepts and declares variable values, performs an operation, and returns a variable.

Properties:

Properties are individual item characteristics defined for an Application.

Proprietary:

Proprietary information is business sensitive information that is sometimes protected by law. For example, a user should be careful when emailing information related to a secret project being worked on within the company.

Push And Pop:

In accounting a LIFO structure means that inventory sales are assessed using the last sales prices first and FIFO would mean sales are assessed using the first sales prices first. In terms of a push and pop data structures in computer science, data is pushed onto a "stack" and it is then popped off in a LIFO style operation. A pop occurs when the amount of values is decremented and the value is removed. Most computer software arrays work using a FIFO style operation.

References:
1. http://en.wikipedia.org/wiki/Stack_(abstract_data_type)
2. Lita Epstein, Reading Financial Reports For Dummies, 2nd Edition, John Wiley & Sons, Inc.
2009 p. 82-83

PVCS:

The Polytron Version Contol System is used to control programming object revisions through the life cycle of a project. It maintains multiple versions of the objects so code can be rolled back or used in a variety of different ways.

Quality Testing and Customer Review:

During the process of software development, after the design, and developer unit test occurs, quality testing occurs when the customer representative tests the code to see if it performs the desired task(s). Having the customer review the changes and sign off on them will protect the developer team to some degree from implementing something that is not useful or potentially damaging for a company.

QuickTime:

This application is used to play movies and songs on a computer and over the Internet.

Radio Group:

A radio group is a group of values on a form that toggle to one selection at a time. For instance, a user might have to choose between male, female, or an unspecified gender.

Reconcile:

Reconcile is used with medical records and bank account records. One set of data entry form values will be compared to a second keying (usually by another user) to ensure they match. This way the company verifies that all of the information was keyed accurately.

Recursion:

Recursion is used when a program continues to call itself and perform a task on an object until a specific event occurs.

Example:

In this Oracle example a recursive program continues deleting data from a specified point in a sample table until it removes all of the duplicates. Note that all of the book titles must be inserted in order into the table.

```
CREATE TABLE vExample (key NUMBER, title VARCHAR2(100));
INSERT INTO vExample Values(1,'BIBLE ');
INSERT INTO vExample Values(2,'CAT ON A ROOF');
INSERT INTO vExample Values(3,'CAT ON A ROOF');
INSERT INTO vExample Values(4,'HORSE TRAINER');
INSERT INTO vExample Values(5,'HORSE TRAINER ');
INSERT INTO vExample Values(6,'JOAN OF ARK');
COMMIT;

CREATE OR REPLACE PROCEDURE remove_duplicateItems
(i NUMBER, i2 NUMBER) AS
  vTitle1 VARCHAR2(100);
  vTitle2 VARCHAR2(100);
BEGIN
  SELECT title INTO vTitle1 FROM vExample WHERE key = i;
  SELECT title INTO vTitle2 FROM vExample WHERE key = i2;
  IF (vTitle1 = vTitle2) THEN
    DELETE FROM vExample WHERE key = i2;
    COMMIT;
```

```
   IF i = 1 THEN
     return;
   ELSE
    remove_duplicateItems(i-2, i-1);
   END IF;
 ELSE
   IF i > 1 THEN
     remove_duplicateItems(i-1, i);
   ELSE
      return;
   END IF;
 END IF;
 END;
DECLARE
BEGIN
 remove_duplicateItems('vExample', 5, 6);
END
```

References:
1.
http://stackoverflow.com/questions/5958566/remove-duplicate-chars-from-a-string-recursively
2.
https://docs.oracle.com/cd/B19306_01/appdev.102/b14261/collections.htm

---

Refresh:

Refresh is a tool found in many applications and tools. It can be used to do things like refresh the latest data in a DB or files on an OS.

Regular Expressions:

Regular Expressions are used in many different programming areas. They can match an alpha numeric pattern in various places like in a DB, on a form, or on a Computer Network address schema. They are applicable to artificial intelligence because humans are very good at recognizing patterns. This is one reason we can remember seemingly unrelated objects in our dreams and recognize friendly or not so friendly patterns from our past. See Regular Expressions in the Database chapter.

Remedy:

This tool is used to assign and track tickets for support techs, developers, and other employees.

Remote Desktop:

Remote Desktop allows users to control or view programs on a remote computer. See pcAnywhere.

Tip:

If the second Remote Desktop monitor becomes hidden run the mstsc /span command on some Operating Systems to display it again.

Reference:
http://superuser.com/questions/99234/remote-desktop-with-multi-monitor-support-in-xp

Tip:

To enable remote access, go to Control Panel, System, Remote, and click on the option to allow users to remotely access the computer.

Retirement Calculator:

These applications can be found on the Internet. They allow users to plug in their current investment input and output information and then calculate how much money they will acquire over time.

REST:

This stands for Representational State Transfer. See REST in the .NET chapter. This protocol specifies tags and security measures for representing data passed around from different resources in different formats across a group of computers and primarily across the Internet. It features a common, stateless interface that is cacheable. It also defines specifications for securely passing data as needed across clients and servers at various system layers.

Reference:
http://www.restapitutorial.com/lessons/whatisrest.html

SAS:

SAS stands for Statistical Analysis Software. This suite of tools was developed by SAS Institue and is used for high performance / high quality data analysis and statistical research. See www.sas.com for addition information.

Save:

The save command is used to save the object a user is working with. It is usually found in the first or second menu header group in an application such as Microsoft Word or Excel.

Screen Cover:

A transparent screen cover is placed over a monitor to make it look less bright. It is used to help developers or users with sensitive eyes.

Screen Shot:

A user can click the print screen or ctrl + print screen button to take a snap shot of the monitor or a piece of the monitor. Then the person can use ctrl + v later to paste the picture in a document or imaging tool.

Screen Saver:

A screen saver will display a darker picture on the computer monitor when it has been idle for a certain amount of time. This protects the monitor bulb from going bad. A security password can be configured so that users have to login before using the computer again.

Service Agreement:

This is an agreement made with a service provider like an Internet Service provider that explains the customer and client obligations behind the service contract.

Server:

There are many different types of servers. They provide services and tools used by Clients computers on the Network. Here is a run down of some of the popular servers that are available:

1. Active Directory Server
2. Microsoft SQL Server
3. Microsoft IIS Web Server
4. Microsoft Office SharePoint Server
5. Oracle Report Server

Set:

This designation is quite often used at the beginning of a function or procedure when setting data values via the calling program. Sometimes the value change occurs right away especially if there is a commit in the program. Other times the data is stored in a container and the value is committed at some point in the future. Developers will see this designation at times in .NET, Java, and Oracle code etc. See Get above.

Single Sign On:

This security feature is offered in Microsoft and Oracle products. It allows the user to login one time through a tool such as Microsoft Active Directory and after that the user can seamlessly move from one application to another within the single sign on infrastructure. It is comparable to using a single card key to gain access to every room within a building.

SnagIt:

The SnagIt tool is used to select a piece of an image and determine its location and size in various units. This tool can be used to set link locations on HTML pages when creating an HTML based prototype, tutorial, or presentation.

Sound Recorder:

The sndrec32.exe is used to record and modify sounds.

SOAP:

This stands for Simple Object Access Protocol. See SOAP under .NET.

Speech Recognition:

Speech Recognition can be setup on some Operating Systems so that the computer recognizes voice commands and performs them.
The picture below shows the Control Panel area in Windows 2000 where Speech Recognition can be setup.

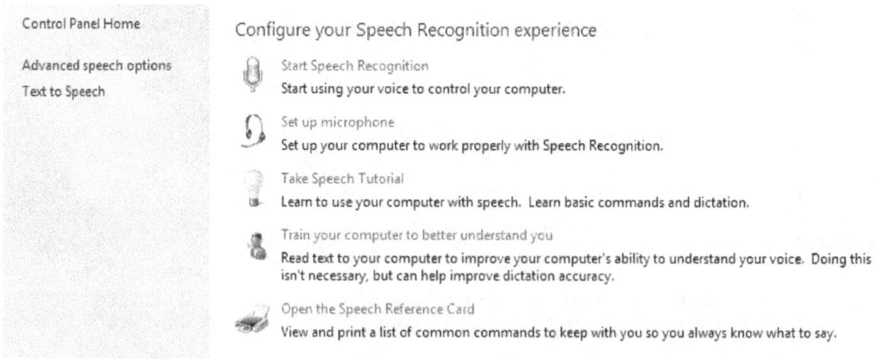

State Chart Diagram:

The State Chart Diagram is used to describe the "off and on" state or functionality of the program. It will display every possible "State" that the program goes through in logical order using arrows and Finite State illustrations. When the user logs in, the program is said to be in an open state. When the program finishes and the user logs out, the program is said to be in a closed state.

Reference:
John W. Satzinger, Robert B. Jackson, Stephen D. Burd, Object-Oriented Analysis and Design with the Unified Process, Cengage Learning, 2004, p.236-246

Struct:

A Struct is a variable used in C# and other C languages. This is a small collection of related facts. It is used somewhat like a lookup table in Excel. It can be used to track the size, shape, and color of an object for example.

Substring:

This function takes a string and a starting position and an ending position and returns the values between these two locations.

Subversion:

Subversion is a free tool used to control and store both old and new software versions. The version control piece integrates with Tortoise SVN on the client side to provide additional functionality. See the subversion.apache.org/ website for additional information.

Swift:

This programming language uses a variation of the C# language in order to build robust apps that function with the iOS and iOS X platforms. iOS and iOS X are both iphones provided by Apple. This falls into the realm of Mobile Programming. A different set of tools

and technology is used to develop Mobile Apps. Learn more about Swift development at https://developer.apple.com/swift.
Also read Learning Swift by O'Reilly Media to learn more about this subject. IDEs like Android Studio or Eclipse produce these mobile Swift Apps. Firechat, Swift Chat, and Swift Weather are examples.

System Table:

A System Table is an underlying DB table that is used to store general information about users, permissions, tables, and other objects in the System.

System Variable:

These can be found in a UNIX operating system. They are used to set environmental variable information specific to the user or system.

Text Item:

A Text Item is an alpha numeric item used in forms and reports and documents.

Terminal Server:

This is a lightweight computer that can be hooked up to a Network and used for purposes like the remote troubleshooting of Network devices.

Reference:
http://en.wikipedia.org/wiki/Terminal_server

Test Track:

This tool is used to assign and track tickets for support techs, developers, and other employees.

Thin Client:

Google: A **thin client** is a lightweight computer that is purpose-built for remote access to a server (typically cloud or desktop virtualization environments). It depends heavily on another computer (its server) to fulfill its computational roles.

Thread:

Coding threads are used to run separate multi-threaded processes in an Application. For instance, one thread may be used to display data on a form, and another thread may be used to aquire user input or enter a sleep state.

Time Zones:

Some computer technology such as schedulers and email software will need to determine what time zones the users operate in. They may need to consider daylight savings time as well. Tools like the one found at www.timeanddate.com/worldclock/converter.html allow developers to convert between time zones. Visual Studio.NET and other IDEs have related libraries that can provide time zone functionality. For instance, in .NET, the timezoneinfo.ConvertTime method can be used to convert from one time to another when associated users exist in different time zones.

Topology Map:

Topology maps are used to track the physical and logical items used within a computer network.

Reference:
Allan Reid, Jim Lorenz, Cheryl Schmidt, Introducing Routing and Switching in the Enterprise, CCNA Discovery Learning Guide, Cisco Press, Apr 25, 2008, Chapter 2

TortoiseSVN:

This client software integrates with Subversion to provide client side version control functionality. Some features this tool provides are a file comparison (DIFF) tool for two files, and a tool that allows users to control file versions without logging in to Subversion. See http://tortoisesvn.Net/ for additional information.

The Waterfall Method of Programming:

This is a technique that some teams use to design software. It starts at the top of the "waterfall" where the software design takes places. It then travels down to the development process, and after that, unit testing and quality testing occurs.

Unified Modeling Language (UML):

With this language developers are allowed to draw out complicated system designs and, in many circumstances, use the language to generate the code.

Unit Test:

A Unit Test occurs when a developer tests his or her code before passing it to the customer representative for additional quality testing.

Use Case Scenarios:

The Use Case documentation describes each piece of an application as well as the user functionality. For example, if developers are building a scheduler the use cases will list each user: ie. the administrator, the participants, and outside viewers, and it will describe all of their capabilities with a certain level of detail.

VBA:

VBA stands for Visual Basic For Applications. This programming language is used in many Microsoft products to manipulate data, navigate through an application, and interact with other products.

VBS:

VBS stands for Visual Basic Script. VBS is a powerful tool used often to automate tasks in a Microsoft Operating. VBS can open applications, perform directory and file tasks, and even check system events. The archive found at http://blogs.technet.com/b/heyscriptingguy/archive/tags/vbscript/ provides a lot of examples of VBS functionality.

Use caution when using VBS! A hacker can manipulate Visual Basic Scripts to do nasty things with an Operation System.

Varidesk:

Veridesk is a computer desk that folds or rises as the user desires.

Web Service:

A Web Service is a Service on the web providing DB or file system information. The accessing application does not need to know how the data is stored on the other end. The program just makes the connection and pulls the data over in a tables or list or other container. Once the developer connects to the Web Service, it will provide information about what can be accessed and how it can be accessed. For example, Amazon provides a Web Service with a lists of products and prices.

Winzip:

Winzip is a tool used to mathematically shrink a file to a smaller size and the extract the file contents later.

Note: There is a command line utility for winzip that can be called from a .NET console job. This is useful if developers want to use code to call the utility and zip files up with a secure password and then unzip them using another application statement.

Wildcards:

Wildcards are filter expressions used to locate specific information in a file or Database. For example, %ing could be used to find words ending with the ing phrase.

XML:

XML stands for Extended Markup Language. It uses file tags to represent data and types as in a table. See XML under Oracle.

XML Spy:

XML Spy allows developers to open, create, and update an XML file.

Yesware:

Yesware allows a company to track how email and links are being used and is generally used for sales purposes. Google Gmail and www.yesware.com feature this technology. See Adware under security for a semi-related topic.

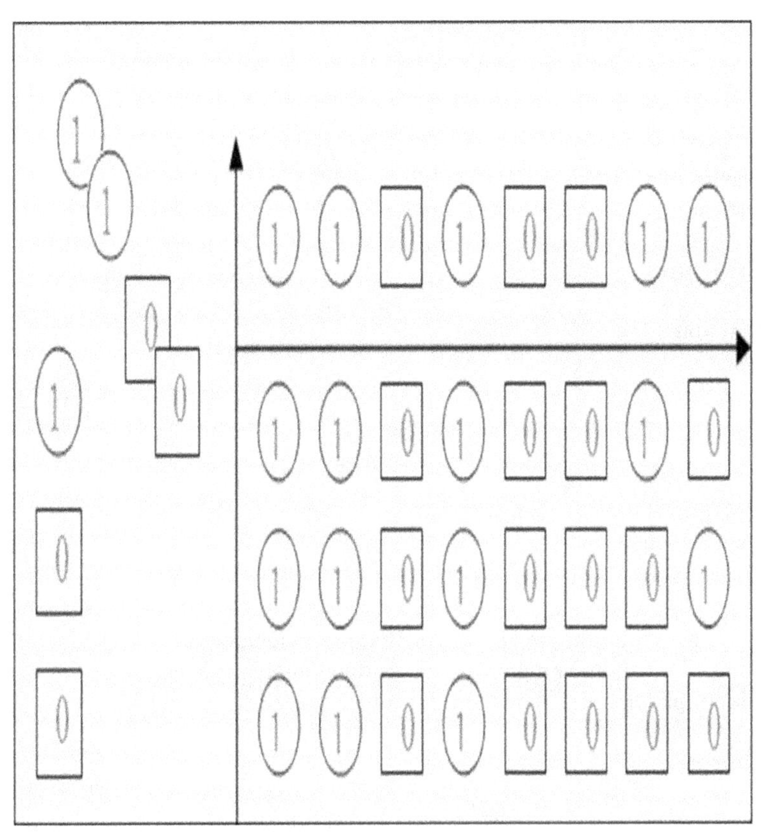
1
1
0
1
0
0
0
1 1 0 1 0 0 1 1
1 1 0 1 0 0 1 0
1 1 0 1 0 0 0 1
1 1 0 1 0 0 0 0

Algorithms

In this chapter:

1. **Bigram**
2. **BTree Assortments**
2. **Bubble Sort**
3. **Dijkstra**
4. **Discrete Structures**
4. **Greedy**
5. **Enigma Machine**
6. **Fuzzy Logic**
7. **Hashing**
8. **Heap**
9. **Logic**
10. **Trigram**
11. **Turing Machine**

Bigram:

A bigram is a two position-grouping of letters. Examples include "NL", "VT", and "TV". Some programs with artificial intelligence use bigrams to look for patterns and store them for future analysis.

BTree Assortments:

When a computer program creates a BTree assortment it looks for a root value and then assigns individual leaves to nodes within the tree. So if a developer has 9 numbers and wants to create a BTree Assortment, he or she will begin by looking at the first number assigning a possible left and right leaf. The figure below shows how the leaves and nodes are inserted. If two numbers are assigned to a left or right node then the largest number will move up and the remaining numbers will split. See step four and nine below for example. Once the tree nodes have been completely inserted this structure makes it easy for a computer program to use an object such as a structure or an array to search through the values, updating and inserting new values. See http://en.wikipedia.org/wiki/B-tree for additional information.

1, 7 , 8 , 14, 9, 15, 21, 20, 17 **Insertion 1:** 1, 7 **Insertion 2:** 7, 8 1 **Insertion 3:** 7 1 8 **Insertion 4:** 7 1 8, 14 **Insertion 5:** 7 9, 14 1 8	**Insertion 6:** 7 14, 15 1 8 9 **Insertion 7:** 7 14 1 8 9 15, 21 **Insertion 8:** 14 7 15 1 8 21 9 **Insertion 9:** 14 7 15 1 8 20, 21 9	**Insertion 10:** 14 7 15, 21 1 8 20 9 **Insertion 11:** 14 7 21 2 8 20 9 15, 17 **Insertion combo step12:** 14 7 21 2 8 17 22 9 15 20

This sorting technique will continue to compare number pairs until an entire list is sorted.

Example: The following example uses Bubble Sort to sort cells in an Excel Spreadsheet. See the Microsoft Word Macro example under File Types and Tools for instructions on how to run macros.

Steps:

1. Create a MS Spreadsheet that looks like this:

	A	B
1	3	
2	5	
3	4	
4	1	
5	2	

1. Create an Excel Macro that looks like this:

```
Sub Bbl_Sort()
'
' Bbl_Sort Macro
' Macro recorded 8/25/2014 by garrissp
' A traditional program will go through RecordCount-1 times to sort all
the values.  In this 'procedure the last two values are calculated
simultaneously.  The second iteration below could be 'made recursive
by using a different technique to pass and store the new values.

'  Go through a few iterations to sort the values

    Dim i As Integer
    Dim NumberRecs As Integer
    Dim lastCell As Integer
    Dim smallest As Integer

    i = Range("A5").Value
    NumberRecs = 5
    'Compare every pair finding the maximum number
    For a = 1 To NumberRecs
        If i < Cells(a, 1) Then
          i = Cells(a, 1)
          lastCell = i
        End If
    Next a

    Range("B5") = i
    'The second iteration.
    'Compare the next set of pairs finding the next max.
```

```
  i = Range("B5").Value
  lastCell = Range("A5").Value
  For a = 1 To (NumberRecs)
   If Cells(a, 1) >= lastCell And Cells(a, 1) < Range("B5").Value
Then
    If Cells(a, 1) >= lastCell Then
     i = Cells(a, 1)
     lastCell = i
    Else
     i = lastCell
    End If
   End If
  Next a
  Range("C5") = Range("B5").Value
  Range("C4") = i

  'Continue comparing.
  i = Range("C4").Value
  lastCell = Range("A5").Value
  For a = 1 To (NumberRecs)
   If Cells(a, 1) >= lastCell And Cells(a, 1) < Range("C4").Value
Then
    If Cells(a, 1) >= lastCell Then
     i = Cells(a, 1)
     lastCell = i
    Else
     i = lastCell
    End If
   End If
  Next a

  Range("D5") = Range("C5").Value
  Range("D4") = Range("C4").Value
  Range("D3") = i

   'Get the last two values.
  i = Range("D3").Value
  lastCell = Range("A5").Value
  For a = 1 To (NumberRecs)
```

```
    If Cells(a, 1) >= lastCell And Cells(a, 1) < Range("D3").Value
Then
      If Cells(a, 1) >= lastCell Then
       i = Cells(a, 1)
       lastCell = i
      Else
       i = lastCell
      End If
    Else
      smallest = Cells(a, 1)
    End If
  Next a

Range("D5") = Range("D5").Value
  Range("D4") = Range("D4").Value
  Range("D3") = Range("D3").Value
  Range("D2") = i
  Range("D1") = smallest

End Sub
```

---

2. Run the Macro and the result will look like this:

	A	B	C	D
1	3			1
2	5			2
3	4			3
4	1		4	4
5	2	5	5	5

Dijkstra's algorithm:

This algorithm allows programmers to determine the shortest path through a data grid or another network like a transportation system. Learn more about this at http://en.wikipedia.org/wiki/Dijkstra's_algorithm. There are many helpful algorithms to be studied on the Internet. Developers can find tons of related examples in different languages there. A few other algorithms to look for include Binary Tree, Genetic, Maximum Flow, and Turing Machine.

Reference:
Introduction To Algorithms, 2nd Edition, The Massachusetts Institute of Technology, 2001

Discrete Structures:

A computer mathematics discipline studying principles such as the order of operations, logic, and matrix multiplication. Read Discrete Structures: An Introduction to Mathematics for Computer Science for additional information on this topic. The book was written by Norris R. Fletcher in 2002

Greedy Algorithm:

This type of algorithm looks for a quick solution to a problem. For instance, if it is looking for the largest summation within a tree of values it may just look at the first few values going down and use that subset to determine what branch meets the criteria.

Read http://en.wikipedia.org/wiki/Greedy_algorithm to learn more.

Also read the Knapsack example in the chapter on Java in this book.

Enigma Machine Algorithm:

The Enigma Machine was used by the Germans during World War II. It was invented by Arthur Scherbius. It used rotors, a plugboard, and ring settings. Codebooks were used every day to set random start message key positions. Rotors turned like a clock a certain amount every 24 hours.

The operator who sent the message would pick random letters to begin with, and encode a message key from the letters. Then he or she would set that message key as the start position, and transmit that start position with a cipher text and an encoded text message. The person who received the message knew how to use those three pieces of information to set their machine and decipher the information.

See http://en.wikipedia.org/wiki/Enigma_machine for additional information.

Fuzzy Logic:

This is a form of logic that looks for approximations instead of an absolute outcome. Job selection and the determination of age are both "possible examples" of applying fuzzy logic. What did the wild peach say about his origin? It's all a bit fuzzy. ☺

Hashing:

Hashing assigns a useful programming index value for a set of values in a list or table.

Example: The following example uses Hashing to sort names in cells in an Excel spreadsheet. It assigns a number representing the first letter in each name and uses that number to sort the listing.

1. The spreadsheet will initially look like this:

	A
1	Mac
2	Abe
3	Cleo
4	Ben
5	John

2. The following macro will hash the data and use the built in sort to sort the values. See the Microsoft Word Macro example under File Types and Tools for instructions on how to run macros.

```
Sub Hash_Sort()
'
' Hash_Sort Macro
' Macro recorded 8/29/2014 by garrissp
'

'  Assign a hash value to these names

   Dim CharPosition As Integer
   Dim NumberRecs As Integer

   NumberRecs = 5
   'Compare every pair finding the maximum number
   For a = 1 To NumberRecs
     CharPosition = InStr(Cells(a, 1).Value, "A")
     If CharPosition = 1 Then
       Cells(a, 2) = 1
     End If
     CharPosition = InStr(Cells(a, 1).Value, "B")
     If CharPosition = 1 Then
       Cells(a, 2) = 2
     End If
     CharPosition = InStr(Cells(a, 1).Value, "C")
     If CharPosition = 1 Then
       Cells(a, 2) = 3
     End If
     CharPosition = InStr(Cells(a, 1).Value, "J")
     If CharPosition = 1 Then
       Cells(a, 2) = 10
     End If
     CharPosition = InStr(Cells(a, 1).Value, "M")
     If CharPosition = 1 Then
       Cells(a, 2) = 13
     End If
```

```
   Next a

   Columns("B:B").Select
   Range("A1:B5").Sort Key1:=Range("B1"), Order1:=xlAscending,
Header:= _
       xlGuess, OrderCustom:=1, MatchCase:=False,
Orientation:=xlTopToBottom, _
       DataOption1:=xlSortNormal

End Sub
```

---

3. The final spreadsheet result will look like this:

	A	B
1	Abe	1
2	Ben	2
3	Cleo	3
4	John	10
5	Mac	13

Heap:

A Heap is a tree data structure, similar to a Btree, in which the key of the parent node is ordered in a way that considers the child node order. In one Heap Structure, the Parent Node Keys are either equal to the Child Node Keys or greater than Child Node Keys and the Largest Key is located at the Root Level. In the other Heap Structure the Parent Node Keys are equal to Child Node Keys or have values that are less than the Child Node Keys and the Smallest Key is at the Root level. Heaps and Btrees are often used in Database Technology.

Reference:
http://en.wikipedia.org/wiki/Heap_(data_structure)

Logic:

This is a Mathematical and Philosophical discipline that determines the probability of the occurance of an event. It uses scientific analysis, probability, and intelligent operations. In computer terms logic may refer to conditional statements such as If A = 1 and B is TRUE Then C IS TRUE. If you are interested in programming and have the money and the time to read, it would be illogical to disregard this book! ☺

Trigram:

A trigram is a three position-grouping of letters. Examples include INL, VIT, and TIV. See bigram above.

Turing Machine Algorithm:

This hypothetical machine was conceived by Alan Turing in the 1930s. The future machine would use an infinite amount of slides. It would cycle through the slides and use "action tables" with preset instructions to decide what to do with the current state or slide. Some of the preset instructions included moving the head, taking on a new state, or writing and erasing symbols. The Turing Machine was theoretically able to accomplish many of the operations of modern day machines. However, it did not take into account some of the complex modern day computing problems such as how and where to store variables, what to do when something unexpected occurs, and how to process requests simultaneously and efficiently.

See http://en.wikipedia.org/wiki/Turing_machine for charts and additional information regarding the Algorithm this hypothetical machine was going to use. According to
http://singularityhub.com/2011/04/04/kurzweil-is-confident-machines-will-pass-turing-test-by-2029-video-2/
some people believe a working Turing Machine will be built in the next few decades.

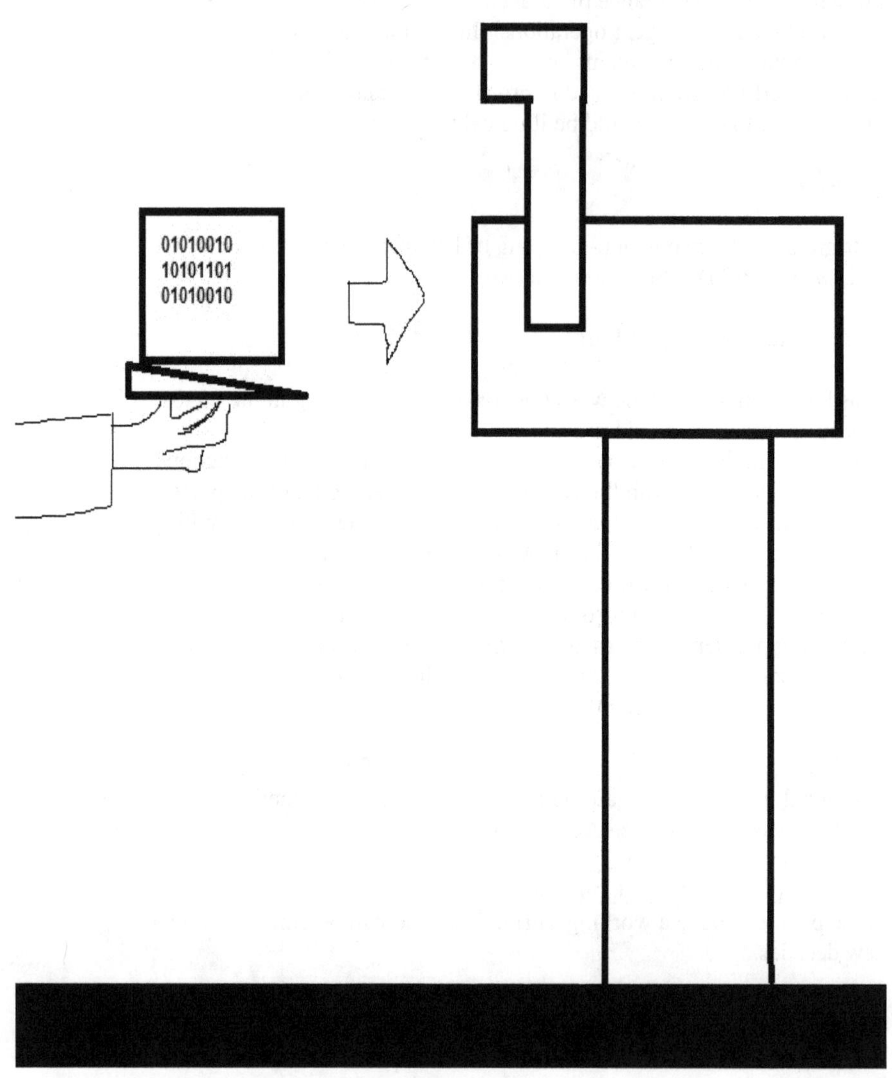
01010010
10101101
01010010

Email

In this chapter:

1. **BCC and CC**
2. **ClickYes Pro 2010**
3. **Distribution List**
4. **Email**
5. **SMS**
6. **SMTP**

Bcc and CC:

Blind Carbon Copy is used to email a person displaying email addresses in the To and CC sections of the email and hiding unspecified addresses in the BCC section. CC stands for Carbon Copy. This is used when an email is primarily intended for one party but other specified recipients may need to be aware of the message.

ClickYes Pro 2010:

Microsoft Outlook has security alerts that require a user to verify if he or she wants to do tasks like sending emails. Some applications, like those used to alert health care providers via an email, may need to bypass these alerts. ClickYes Pro 2010 can be called from a program and used to automatically accept these security warnings.

Distribution List:

A Distribution List is a list of email addresses. When a user selects a Distribution List, and sends an email to it, everyone in the Distribution List receives the email.

Email:

Email stands for Electronic Mail. It is basically the computer alternative to sending mail through the post office.

Important Note: There are some email related concepts that are not learned in classrooms. For instance, one should not fire off a quick bolded email text with angry words or use terms like ASAP and problematic. Emails should not be used as an alternative to face to face meetings or instant message to chat between one or more people. Sometimes it is better to communicate ideas directly, on the phone, or via IM because emails can be forwarded or used for political purposes. It is also important to consider what you are sending, and ensure it is not sensitive or proprietary information that should be intended for another destination.

Programmers utilize objects like the PKG_EMAIL package in Oracle to email application data as needed. Microsoft code like VBA macros that call SMTP (Simple Mail Transfer Protocol) centered functions can also be used to email clients text messages and attachments. There are a variety of Servers that host Email. Some Email Server examples are listed below:

AOL: America Online offers a free email server. See www.aol.com to learn more about this free Internet service.

Gmail: Gmail is provided by Google. See www.gmail.com to learn more about this free Internet service. Gmail has service plugins that extend its functionality. For example, Yesware is a plugin that allows sales people to track who is corresponding with them.

Microsoft Hotmail: This is a free tool offered by Microsoft. See www.hotmail.com to learn more about this free Internet service.

Microsoft Outlook: This is another Email Server application. Learn more about Microsoft Outlook at en.wikipedia.og/wiki/Microsoft_Outlook.

Yahoo: Yahoo offers a free email tool as well. See www.yahoo.com to learn more about this free Internet service.

Tip:

Code such as C# or VBA can be used with protocols like the Simple Mail Transfer Protocol to mimic actions such as creating, sending, and organizing emails. This is very helpful if and when email automation is necessary. Note that the developer should be careful when automating emails to put in some kind of catch in case a glitch occurs and the email is sent out over and over again.

Keep in mind, Email messages are not generally secure. Tools such as Wireshark are able to intercept these messages unless extensive security measures have been taken by the Developer.

Read more about email technology and security online and in various books like Security Power Tools published by O'Reilly Media.

SMS:

Short Message Service is a Protocol that works with mobile devices to send quick message between the devices.

Reference:
www.ehow.com/list_6533654_list-sms-email-extensions.html

SMTP:

Simple Mail Transfer Protocol is a Protocol used to specify Email information like a Subject, Recipient, and Message, and send it out successfully.

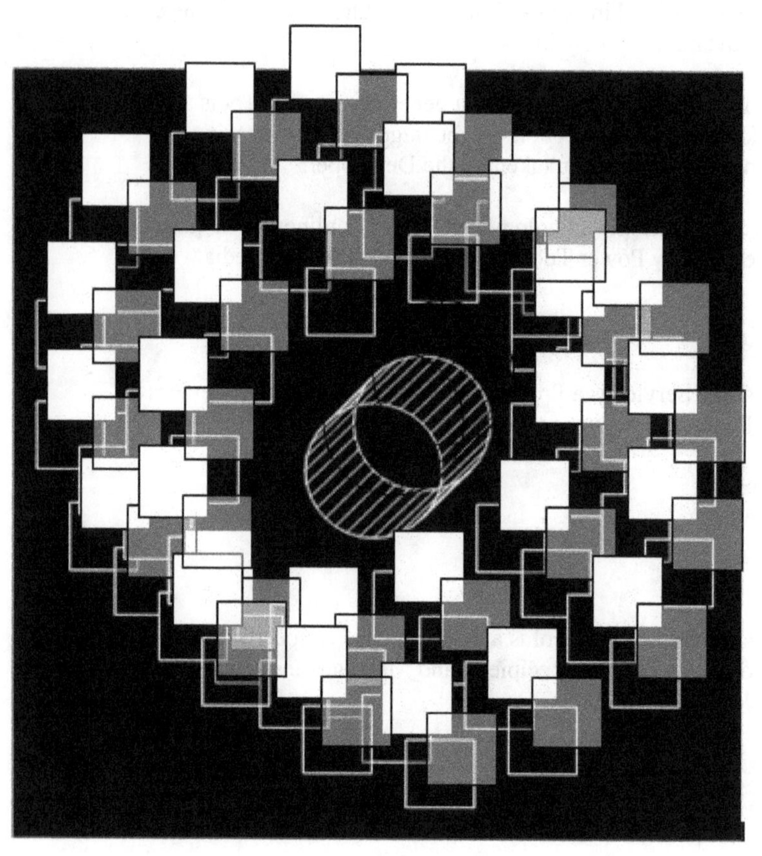

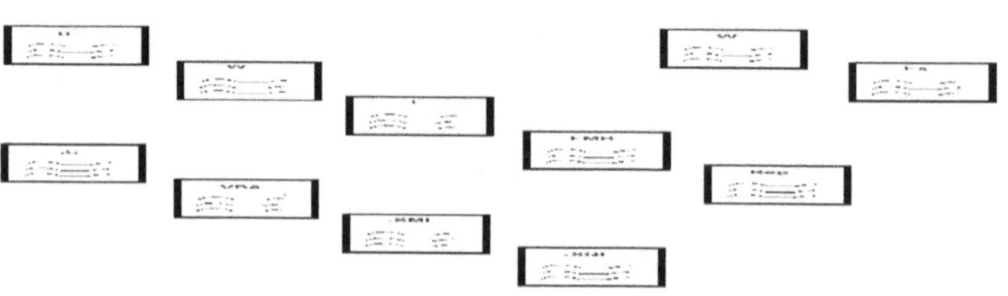

File Types And Tools

In this chapter:

1. **File Types**
2. **Tools And Concepts**

File Types

aspx:

This is an Active Server Page extension as discussed in the .NET chapter above.

avi:

This is an Audio Video Interleave file used by multimedia players.

css:

Cascading Style Sheets are like templates for HTML files. Developers can add things like background colors for frames, fonts for menus and titles, and other formatting specifications.

Take a look at http://www.w3schools.com/css/css_examples.asp for additional examples and guidelines.

Example:

This is an example website including an applet and a cascading style sheet to set the background color. Save this as index.html and open it in a browser to see how it works.

```
<HTML>
<HEAD>
<STYLE>
BODY {
   background-color: #99FF99;
}
```

```
</STYLE>
<TITLE><H1> Our Website </H1></TITLE>
</HEAD>
<BODY>

<h2>A Helpful Message:</h2>
<APPLET CODE="Greetings.class" WIDTH=150 HEIGHT=25>
</APPLET>
<h3>See http://www.w3schools.com/tags/ref_colorpicker.asp for a
helpful color chart.</h3>
</BODY>
</HTML>
```

---

csh:

The Corn Shell Script allows developers to create scripts using various Linux and Korn Shell commands. See the Csh and Sh Scripts section under Unix and Linux commands in the Unix and Linux chapter.

csv:

A comma separated file uses commas to separate column values. Be careful importing these into Excel. For instance, if there are extra commas within character fields, and the user imports using a comma delimiter, the data may be moved over to a new column. If this happens, use a tab delimiter alternative to specify where the next column occurs.

HTML:

Hypertext Markup language is the primary language used to create websites on the Internet. It allows Developers to incorporate a variety of foreground and background colors, links, images, text formatting, tables, headers, borders, linked sections, templates through XML skins, et cetera. See css above.

fmb:

See Oracle Forms under Oracle.

js:

Java script sections or separate java script pages are used along with HTML code to provide additional functionality within a website. For instance, functions may be used to change colors, move users to a different section in a page, or change button icons to show they have been used. Take a look in the Legislation chapter, at the Section 508 section titled Examples For How To Be And How Not To Be Compliant. See the 6th example in this section. Also see www.w3schools.com/js/ for a good tutorial with examples on this subject.

jsp:

A Java Server Page script has two parts. One part interacts with data on the server and the other part works with the website HTML interface for the client. This separation of responsibilities makes jsp a robust and efficient language for developing projects.

Tip:

A JSP stack trace will display on some web browsers like Mozilla Firefox if an error occurs. This allows developer to troubleshoot problems more effectively.

mmb:

A mmb is an Oracle Forms Menu object. The various menus can be setup and the code behind will handle the navigation.

Tip:

Oracle places an underline under the first letter of each mmb menu option as a hot key for navigating. However, this property can be overwritten by placing an & beside the letter the developer wants to choose as the hot key.

Tip:

If a developer is unsure what the name of a virtual Oracle form is, he or she can look in the triggers behind the mmb menu screen to determine the actual fmb name needing analysis or modification.

Mp4:

A Mp4 is typically used to store audio and video data and to play and display it with a multimedia player.

olb:

This stands for Oracle Library. It contains reusable PL/SQL code pieces used within programs like Oracle Forms..

rdf:

See Oracle Reports under Oracle.

Wmv:

Windows Media Video files contain audio and video media for various multimedia playing tools.

Tools and Concepts

File Comparison:

Developers sometimes use a file comparison tool to determine the difference between two or more files. Tortoise SVN is a good freeware tool used for this purpose.

Once the Tortoise SVN is installed, developers will notice a Diff menu option when right clicking two files in the OS. If they click on Diff it will show them the two files beside each other and allow them to cycle through any differences between the files. They can compare the files by first holding down the shift key to select them with the left mouse click, and then right clicking one file, and selecting the subversion comparison option. The tool can be downloaded at tortoisesvn.net.

grep:

Developers use grep to search for a regular expression in one or more selected directories on the computer. There is also a Windows version of the Linux grep tool called Grep 32.

grep32:

This is the Windows version of the Linux grep tool. See Grep above.

HTML:

HTML stands for Hypertext Markup Language. It is used to develop browser hosted websites and it is compatible with other programming languages such as javascript, jquery, jsp, and aspx. See www.w3schools.com/html for a great tutorial on this subject. HTTP or Hypertext Transfer Protocol is a Protocol used to transfer HTML pages across the Internet. Some common HTTP error messages that developers might encounter are:

> Error 400: The programming request was not made properly so it was a "bad request".

Error 401: The user is "unauthorized" to access the content.

Error 403: The website is "forbidden" and does not allow a access of any kind.

Error 404: The website was "not found".

Error 500: There was an "internal server error".

Hosting A Website:

A web hosting company such as www.godaddy.com or another company has to perform several steps to host a website. Some of these steps include:

1. Setting up a server without outside access to the Internet.
2. Setting up security such as a firewall for the internal network.
3. Obtaining a domain name from a Domain Name Registrar. See http://en.wikipedia.org/wiki/Domain_name_registrar for details.
4. Setting up DNS and other IP address settings so the server will become accessible on the Internet.
5. Setting up a file transfer program on the server so files can be uploaded.
6. Considering the setup of other Internet Development tools and services such as Adobe Connect, Outlook, and MySql.
7. Advertizing their services et cetera.
8. Doing everything possible to ensure 24 hour access to websites.

Read more about hosting a website in the Website Hosting for Dummies book.

IM:

Instant Messaging tools like Pidgin and Google Talk allow users to carry on text based conversations across a Network or the Internet. See Email.

LINQ:

When creating Microsoft .NET applications developers can use the Language Integrated Query language to select and manipulate information from data sets, XML documents, and conventional databases. To learn more, take a look at the examples found at http://code.msdn.microsoft.com/101-LINQ-Samples-3fb9811b.

Linux Commands:

The Linux OS and Unix OS have many useful Linux commands. See http://www.computerhope.com/unix.htm for more information. Here is a small list of these commands and what they do:

Cat – Used to display file content on the monitor.
clear – To clear the monitor.
Cal– To display the system calendar.
Date: To see the system date.
Dir – To see the contents of a directory.
find / -name init.ora – To find a file.
Finger – To see the System users.
Grep – See Grep above.
Ls – To list files in a directory.
Up Arrow – To cycle historical commands.
Vi – To start the visual text editor.

Microsoft Access:

Users use Microsoft Access to create, modify, and query tables, setup forms and reports, and interact with other programs. An Access VBA Macro or referenced Module can be used to do things like open a Word Document and add table data content inside in a logical way. See http://allenbrowne.com/ser-29.html and the example of writing to a document at http://stackoverflow.com/questions/24031426/using-ms-access-and-vba-to-generate-ms-word-document for additional information.

Microsoft Excel:

Excel groups data pieces into workbooks and worksheets. A workbook groups similar worksheets together to provide mathematical information such as accounting information or statistical information. Functions and tools within Excel allow users to manipulate data. The following is a list of some functions, tools, and concepts the author uses when working in Excel.

Cells:

A cell is the intersection of a row and a column in a worksheet.

Rows and Columns:

Remember RC. Rows are records going horizontally across a worksheet. Columns are a vertical group of fields on a worksheet.

Worksheets:

These individual pages contain information about a specific piece of information like the cost of breakfast foods in 2014.

Tip:

Worksheet Cells can reference other Workbooks and Worksheet Cells.

Workbooks:

A Workbook is a collection of related Worksheets.

Excel Functions:

Users can incorporate functions within a cell formula to do things like averaging and summing values. Here are a few function examples:

> AVG: Calculates a field value average.
>
> MATCH: Determines if a field value match occurs.

SUM: Calculates a field value summation.

VLookUp: Looks up a value from a list of values.

Macro Recordings and Modules:

When a developer clicks the Macro – Record New Macro item the workbook will record every use action using a VBA script. He or she can later go to Macro – Macros to rerun the functionality or to view the script, make changes to it, and learn how the VBA works. Modules can also be created to maintain frequently used code that is commonly used within one or more Macros. See Macros under Microsoft Word for additional information.

Example:

Using the VBA Input Box:

An Input Box queries for and accepts user input in a Macro or Module. This line example asks for a number and assigns it to myNumber.

myNumber = Application.InputBox("Give me a number:")

Reference:
http://msdn.microsoft.com/en-us/library/office/ff839468(v=office.15).aspx

Example:

Pivot tables:

Pivot tables allow users to summarize row and column data within a spreadsheet.

The following screenshots show how to summarize a row and a column of data to create a Pivot table in Microsoft Excel:

Step 1: Create the following table.
Highlight the rows and columns to pivot on.

Employee	Year	Item	Number Sold
1	2001	100	50
1	2001	200	40
2	2001	100	70
3	2001	100	50
1	2002	100	20
2	2002	100	30
1	2003	200	50
1	2004	300	10
2	2004	100	150
3	2004	200	40
4	2004	300	50
5	2004	400	60

Step 2: Choose the Pivot Table and Pivot Chart Report.

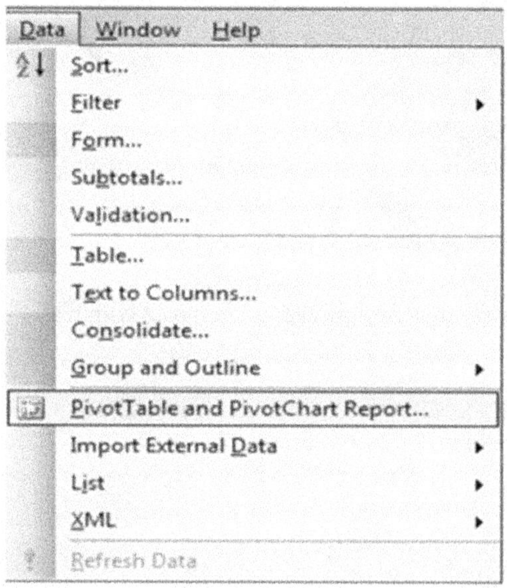

Step 3: Leave the defaults selected in the Wizard Steps 1 and 2 and click on Next.

Step 4: Click on Layout. Drag the Employee to the Row field, drag the Year and Item to the Column field, and drag the Number Sold into the Data field. Click OK.

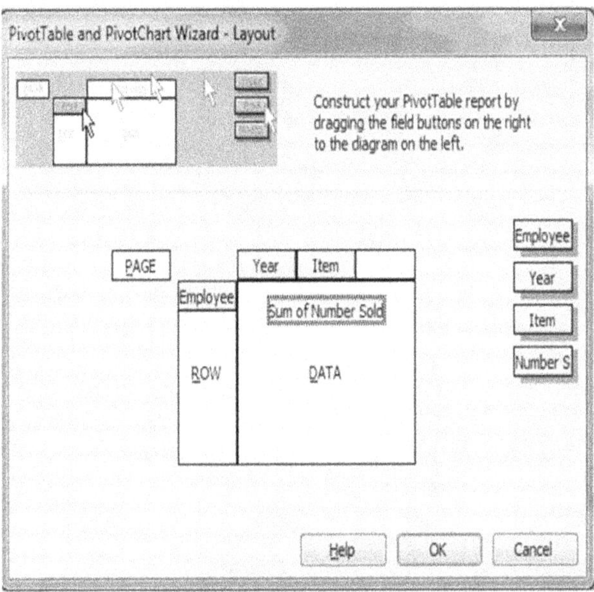

Step 5: Click Finish to create the following worksheet. Note that it shows the total number of items sold per year for each employee. The results can be rerun at any point.

Drop Page Fields Here

Sum of Number Sold	Year / Item												
	2001		2001 Total	2002	2002 Total	2003	2003 Total	2004				2004 Total	Grand Total
Employee	100	200		100		200		100	200	300	400		
1	50	40	90	20	20	50	50			10		10	170
2	70		70	30	30			150				150	250
3	50		50						40			40	90
4										50		50	50
5											60	60	60
Grand Total	170	40	210	50	50	50	50	150	40	60	60	310	620

Formula References:

When a Function or tool points to a worksheet item in the workbook that is known as a Formula Reference. For instance if the users types in = within a field and goes to Sheet 2, field C8, he or she will see this in the formula: =Sheet2!C8. That means that the value in the current field will be set to the value in Sheet 2, column C row 8. References refer to objecs such as Rows, Tabs, Workbooks, and Worksheets.

Microsoft InfoPath:

This Microsoft tool allows users to design and modify forms used to display and modify data stored in various locations such as Spreadsheets and Databases. These sofisticted looking forms are similar to the forms created in Access and Excel.

Microsoft SharePoint Portal:

SharePoint is not an all inclusive Database or a Data Warehouse of information. It summarizes Enterprise and multiple Company level information in a personalized way for different people. It includes employee contact information, Web Parts, work flows, and search tags. It is able to integrate with SOAP, REST, Microsoft InfoPath, Excel related languages and products. Users are setup in groups used for security later on down the line. When a user logs in, he or she can view a list of related contacts and Web Parts available to completing a job. Web Parts are used to summarize information and to present it to a secured subset of users.

Data summaries can be pulled from outside sources like Databases and XML files with supporting information stored in SharePoint Lists. Developers can find out more about the difference between lists and DB tables at http://msdn.microsoft.com/en-us/library/ff647105.aspx.

Work flows can be created to alert users when a specific task needs to be completed for a project. Developers are also privy to a sandbox area where they can develop new lists and SharePoint Web Parts without affecting the live production system and the users.

There are several flavors of SharePoint. The Enterprise Edition offers the most powerful set of tools, but it is more expensive. For instance, a company will need this tool set if they want to connect to an outside Database and pull information. If a company does not want to setup the required 64 bit OS Server to host SharePoint it can go through a Cloud provider alternative such as Office 365.

Tip:

SharePoint can only display a certain amount of records.
Read more about this consideration at support.microsoft.com/kb/2759051 and go through the tutorial found at http://office.microsoft.com/en-001/sharepoint-server-help/overview-RZ101874361.aspx?section=1 to learn more about it.

Here are some additional SharePoint terms developers might encounter along the way:

Application Layouts: These are layout templates a Developer can use to produce a Microsoft SharePoint application quickly.

Branding: Incorporating symbols, larger pictures, or even a continuous website border to associate a company or organization with the application is known as branding a website.

Dashboard: This is where a SharePoint person goes to have access to his or her SharePoint Portal functionality. For instance, an admin can use the dashboard to create users, and a CEO can see how much revenue has been generated at a higher company level.

Enterprise Content Management: This concept allows users to collect information with associated tags and use it to search for and update company wide data in an efficient manner.

Groups: SharePoint applications have different groups that users can be added to such as Administrators, Managers, and General Employees.

Lists: Lists are used instead of tables in SharePoint. They still have columns and rows. However, a Portal is suppose to give a birds eye view of company information. So instead of collecting data in a large Database table format, lists are suppose to be smaller and easier to traverse and maintain. http://technet.microsoft.com/en-us/library/cc262787(v=office.15).aspx#ListLibrary states that SharePoint 2013 can have up to 30,000,000 items.

Lookup Fields: This is a list item that pulls from another list.

Metadata: Metadata tag properties are setup to associate and describe similar items. The various Metadata values allow users to search and update list values quickly and efficiently.

Record Management: Record Management refers to the SharePoint's ability to store information related to employees, contacts, documents, and other business items in a logical and easy to use manner.

REST: SharePoint incorporates REST functionality. See REST in the .NET chapter.

Settings: Sandbox: The name says it all. Developers can play around here until they are ready to implement a fix in Production.

Skins: Skins are predefined layout objects that can be used to introduce a similar look and feel within a SharePoint application. See css under File Types.

TeamSite: A team site is a location on the Portal where team members can collaborate, sharing documents and notes, with different permissions setup for Project related objects.

Templates: Developers can select SharePoint templates to give a similar look and feel to an specific area on the portal.

Themes: A Theme incorporates a collection of fonts, colors, and other Web Site specifications and is used to further the concepts of branding and skinning within a SharePoint portal.

Web Parts: These are objects dropped into a Portal used to perform different tasks and display various data. A Web Part could pull data from a DB if the developer is using the Enterprise SharePoint edition with Connectivity Services. Or it could simply be used to display dates and times and similar information from various SharePoint lists.

Workflows: Workflows are related project events. A SharePoint workflow is assigned to various users and automatically walks them through tasks and steps over time. Workflows are great tools for project managers and teams and they are not too difficult to implement.

Microsoft VBA (Visual Basic For Applications):

VBA is a powerful coding programming-language-tool incorporated within many Microsoft Objects. Developers use VBA macros and modules to loop through Microsoft Excel rows and other Microsoft Objects. They can even loop through containers in MS Access. See containers under Database Objects in the Databast Technology chapter. VBA has many other uses like displaying images, sorting worksheets, and updating files.

Microsoft Word:

Users can create large documents and even books with this program. Some of the illustrations in this book were created using the MS Word 3-D Style tool under the Drawing toolbar. Word can also allow users to track changes, insert images, change fonts, styles, and colors, and adjust various document settings. There are a lot of hidden features in this application. For instance, the Tools –Envelopes and Labels option tool can be used to create business cards and or labels for an envelope.

Creating a Word Document using data from another Microsoft application is another useful feature. There is a write up on how to do this at http://www.ozgrid.com/forum/showthread.php?t=50936 or just search www.google.com for "Use VBA to create a Word Document". Mail Merge is another tool that can be used in Microsoft Word to produce a similar result.

Tip:

If a user type – several times MS Word will create a section border line. To remove the line, using the Professional Edition 2003, put the cursor above the line, go to Format – Borders and Shading, and click None in the Borders section.

Reference:
http://www.pcmag.com/article2/0,2817,485644,00.asp

Tip:

Word has a Translate tool under the Tools – Language menu selection. Use this tool to translate a phrase or an entire document from one language to another. See Google Translate for additional information.

Macros:

Users can go to Tools – Macos record Macro or Edit Macro. The first option will allow them to go through steps and record everything they do. Users can also return to Macros later, select a macro, and run the same steps programatically.

Example:

The Macro below will drop a ball or an "o" from the top of the document to 10 entries below. Open Microsoft Word, type "o" at the beginning of the document, and then go to Macros, Edit Macro, and insert the following:

```
Sub MacroDropBall()
'
' MacroDropBall Macro
' Macro recorded 8/21/2014 by garrissp
'
'The "Do Until time1 >= time2" code was acquired from this website:
'http://stackoverflow.com/questions/1544526/how-to-pause-for-
specific-amount-of-time

Dim time1, time2, first, last

    Application.WindowState = wdWindowStateMaximize
    ActiveWindow.ActivePane.View.Zoom.Percentage = 100
    Selection.TypeText Text:="o"

    first = 1
    last = 10
    Do Until first = last
    time1 = Now
    time2 = Now + TimeValue("0:00:01")
      Do Until time1 >= time2
        DoEvents
        time1 = Now()
      Loop
     Selection.TypeBackspace
     Selection.TypeParagraph
     Selection.TypeText Text:="o"
    first = first + 1
    Loop

End Sub
```

Test this out by going to Macros, clicking the edited Macro, and clicking Run.

Tip:

The help tool in the Microsoft Office suite is very useful. For instance, if a user wants to know how to disable and enable Macros, he or she can click on Help search for "Macro Security.

Oracle

In this chapter:

1. Oracle Tools

Oracle is a powerful and robust company offering many tools for hosting and developing effective applications. These tools offer great support for secure Database and Website development as well as the development of off line-stand alone business related projects.

Oracle Tools

The following is a list of some of the business tools Oracle has to offer.

Oracle Application Development Framework:

The Java based JDeveloper and Application Development Framework, as well as the Oracle Application Express IDEs have begun to take the place of Oracle Forms and Reports because they are able to produce more advanced web based Oracle applications. These tools are based heavily on Java and PL/SQL coding techniques. Read http://www.oracle.com/technetwork/developer-tools/adf/overview/index.html for additional information. See http://docs.oracle.com/cd/E53569_01/tutorials/tut_rich_app/tut_rich_app.html for an ADF tutorial.

Oracle Application Express:

See Oracle Application Development Framework and read http://www.oracle.com/technetwork/developer-tools/apex/application-express/apex-for-forms-098747.html for additional information.

Oracle Developer:

This IDE allows developers to create software using various Oracle tools such as Forms, Reports, and JDeveloper. All of the tools are integrated into a single environment. Read http://en.wikipedia.org/wiki/Oracle_Developer_Suite for additional information.

Oracle Forms:

Oracle Forms allows Programmers to create Oracle forms related software such as Libraries, forms, record groups, and visual attributes. Even though ADF is becoming more popular it still incorporates Forms technology so it is useful to study. Oracle forms are driven by triggering events that occur at the form, block, and item levels. It is useful to understand the firing order for these triggers and what they do.

Many of the form level triggers fire before the item level triggers. For instance, Pre-Login, When-New-Form-Instance, and When-Form-Activated are some of the first triggers to fire when a form is opened. Post Query, When-Button-Pressed, and When-Validate-Item are some of the first triggers to fire when changes occur in a block or in an item. There are a set of triggers that fire for the overall form, and for the individual blocks. They usually fire in order starting with the higher level groups and going down to the individual items. These triggers will fire and run PL/SQL code in order within each triggering group. http://appselangovan.blogspot.com/2011/06/firing-sequence-of-form-triggers.html provides a listing of Triggers and firing orders.

The following is a list of some Oracle Form Triggers and what they are used for:

Pre-Login: This fires before a user logs into a DB.
Post-Login: This fires after a user logs into a DB.
Pre-Form: This fires before loading a form.
When-Form-Activated: This fires every time a form is activated for use.
When-New-Form-Instance: This fires at the first instantiation of a form.
Pre-Query: This fires before block data is queried.
Pre-Pop-Menu: This fires before the Popup menu appears. It can be used to navigate to an item associated with the menu.
Post-Query: This fires after block data is queried.
When-New-Item-Instance: This fires when a record item is instantiated for the first time.
When-Validate-Item: This fires after an item is changed and the user attempts to move away.

Key-Next: This fires when a user moves to the next item.
Key-Previous: This fires when users move to a previous item.

Blocks are based on their Query Data Source Type and Name properties. These generally select data from a table or a reference cursor. Take a look at the Reference Cursors section below for additional details. Block level joins are used to connect two blocks (and their underlying tables together). Block and item properties are used to determine things like how locks occur, if a scroll bar is shown, and how to navigate between items.
Some useful PL/SQL commands in Oracle Forms include:

```
CALL_ALERT('success or failure','message value');
FIRST_RECORD;  --to go to the first record
LAST_RECORD;
NEXT_RECORD;
SELECT INTO…
GO_BLOCK;
CLEAR_BLOCK;
GET_LIST_ELEMENT_VALUE --to pull a specific list value
GET_ITEM_PROPERTY
SET_RADIO_BUTTON_PROPERTY('BLOCK.RADIO_GR
OUP','ITEM',PROPERTY,PROPERTY_FALSE);
:SYSTEM.CURRENT_ITEM
```

Tip:

If a Developer wants to see if an item has changed (ie. before moving away from a form) one technique is to incorporate a package to store form level values. The package could be called ValuesForASession. The form will set these values when a trigger like a WHEN-NEW-RECORD or a WHEN-VALIDATE trigger fires and then compare the values against the actual block item values before continuing an operation. Remember when comparing two values that may be NULL it is important to use a NVL([FieldName],[Value]) because NULL does not equal NULL in Oracle Forms. NVL will take a field and substitute another value if it is NULL so using NVL(field1,0) + NVL(field2,0) will work when NULL + 2 will probably not work and produce an error.

Code is used within the Triggers to accomplish various tasks. Some tasks include item validation, value calculation, and form navigation.

Tip:

Sometimes code changes the query behind the block. To see what that looks like add a bogus named database item to the block. When the form runs it will error. Then click ctrl + shift + e to see the query.

Example:

The following PL/SQL example returns the user from a data entry form back to a master record form and loops through the records until it finds the record being edited:

```
DECLARE
  vPrimaryKeyFieldValue   [Master Block Table].[PKField]%TYPE;
BEGIN
  vPrimaryKeyFieldValue := [Detail Block].[PKField];
  -- go to the record

  Go_Block([Master Block]);
  Clear_Block;
  Execute_Query;
  First_Record;  --Or use Go_Record(1);
  LOOP
      exit when :[Master Block].[PKKeyField] =
         vPrimaryKeyFieldValue
      OR :SYSTEM.LAST_RECORD = 'TRUE';
      --Get_Block_Property('BlockName',CURRENT_RECORD)
      --will specify what record the cursor is at, i.e. rec. 3, 2, or 1.
      NEXT_RECORD;
  END LOOP;
END;
```

Many items such as list and combo boxes and date fields can be dropped onto an Oracle Form canvas to. As mentioned previously, triggers are used with these items for different purposes.

Tip:

If a Developer needs to delete an item from a Oracle Forms list, in the list item properties, he or she should go to properties, Elements In List, select the unneeded value and click ctrl+shift+< at the same time.

Tip:

Exceptions can be declared and then used to handle problematic situations. For instance, if a user attempts to assign a possible string value to a numeric variable the developer can use a RAISE Exception statement or a Predefined Exception to catch the problem and alert them. See http://docs.oracle.com/cd/E13085_01/doc/timesten.1121/e13076/exceptions.htm for additional information on Predefined Exceptions.

Example:

Some triggers are not able to perform certain actions. For instance, a When-Validate-Item is not allowed to use a GO_ITEM command. When this occurs, a WHEN-TIMER-EXPIRED form level trigger can be used to catch the event and implement the necessary command. The following example uses the WHEN-,TIMER-EXPIRED to allow a validate trigger to go to a form item. Follow these Steps to complete the example:

1. Place a WHEN-TIMER-EXPIRED trigger in a WHEN-VALIDATE-ITEM as shown below.

```
DECLARE

  t_id TIMER;

BEGIN
```

```
IF :BLOCK.FIELD IS NULL THEN
  t_id := CREATE_TIMER('MY_TIMER',100,REPEAT);
END IF;

END;
```

---

2. Create the following WHEN-TIMER-EXPIRED trigger at the form level.

```
DECLARE
 t_id TIMER;
BEGIN
 t_id := find_timer('MY_TIMER');
 IF NOT ID_NULL(t_id) then
   GO_ITEM(' Block.Field');
   DELETE_TIMER(t_id);
 END IF;
END;
```

---

3. To test the WHEN-TIMER-EXPIRED trigger, run the form, change the item value, and move to another item.

Text item navigation is handled by using the GO_ITEM function or it can be setup in the item properties. A developer can choose the Previous and Next navigation items at the field property level.

Tip:

Sometimes a problem will occur with the text item not being highlighted when using a GO_ITEM statement. If this happens, set the keep cursor position property to yes on the item, and use code to go to the Previous_Item and then the NEXT_ITEM.

Tip:

To get help developers can go to the Help menu item and click Use Online Help to find out more about the various trigger possibilities.

Oracle attached libraries include reusable PL/SQL functions, procedures and packages. These can be attached to the Form by clicking the Add Item + under Attached Libraries. It may be necessary to insert these Libraries in the ORACLE_FORMS directory as specified in Regedit. These libraries can add functionality to the form like Java based data validation and alerting mechanisms..

Visual Attributes define the look and feel of an item in Oracle Forms. These attributes are custom made and reusable components.

Record Group are created to select specific information used in the Form. A List of Values (LOV) can be created that will pull data from the Record Group into a list or Combo Box. See http://plaincityblogger.blogspot.com/2010/02/oracle-forms-record-group-processing.html for more details.

Developers may need to restore data back to a particular place in time in Oracle Forms. If this becomes necessary insert a Savepoint [savePoint Name] specifier inside of the PL/SQL code block. After this the developer will be able to run the rollback or commit [savePoint Name] statement to Undo or Save his or her work.

Tip:

If the Oracle Form does not display on the Desktop when opening try the following: Right click on the shortcut, go to properties, and change the Shortcut Run option to Maximized and try it again.

Tip:

If a Developer needs to Serialize information in an Oracle Form he or she can use the XML Serializer package. See http://docs.oracle.com/cd/E13222_01/wls/docs70/javadocs/weblogic/apache/xml/serialize/package-summary.html for additional details.

Oracle Application Testing Software:

This automated testing tool is used to record and perform supplemental tests against an Oracle Application. As with most Oracle tools, this Software does require some setup and configuration. See http://docs.oracle.com/cd/E25292_01/doc.901/e15484/oltchap3.htm for additional information.

Oracle Errors Occurring Frequently:

The following is a list of common Oracle errors and possible solutions:

Form Mutation: If objects within Oracle Forms mutate as a result of being compiled in a later version the best fix for this is to go through each object property and revert it back to the original object type.

FRM-10044: Cannot create file.
The file permissions may be set to read only so it cannot be compiled.

FRM-12001: Cannote create the record group (check your query).
It may be necessary to exit Form Builder, come back in, and try again.

FRM-30049: Unable to build column mapping.
See FRM-30085 below.

FRM-30085: Unable to adjust form for output.
If this error occurs check the Oracle Form triggers to see if there is a BEGIN statement without an End Statement. Also check the Record Group properties. See FRM-32082 for another possible solution.

FRM-30174: Values must be distinct.
If a FRM-30174 error occurs in an Oracle module verify that all the check boxes have their own unique values.

FRM-32082: Invalid value for given item type.
Try to insert a value into the first element of the problematic list or change the Record Group.

FRM-40105: Unable to resolve reference to item XXX.
A JavaBean or other program may be missing and may need to be included in the form canvas, window, and data block.

FRM-40505: Oracle error: Unable to perform query.
This could mean a table and or user permissions are missing. It could also mean the application is referencing an invalid field or object.

FRM-40735: Unhandled exception ORA-04062
This is a catch all error. Verify that the object in question is being compiled correctly.

FRM-41011: Undefined Visual Attribute
This means a visual attribute is undefined. Insert debugs in the start up triggers to see where it is occurring. Insert VA from another form. Note: Try TEXT_ON, TEXT_OFF, GRAYED_OUT, & LINKOFF.

FRM-41039: Invalid Alert.
This means the developer may need to set the title property or another property of an alert within the programming object.

FRM-41331: Could not delete element…
Attempt to change the poplist Database property to No, but continue to allow Inserts and Updates.

FRM0-41337: Cannot populate list…
It may be necessary to properly commit data before accessing list records. Look under Oracle Forms at the Savepoint paragraph.

FRM-41380: Cannot set the blocks query data source.
If this occurs try clearing the block before setting the Query_Data_Source_Name or putting data into the block.

FRM-92101: Field must be entered
This means there is a field that requires a value.

FRM-92091: Unexpected Fatal Error in client-side Java Code.
If a list box is being filled with a large amount of records, try limiting the amount using a statement like Where rownum < a certain number and allow for additional filtering.

FRM-93652: The runtime process has terminated abnormally.
If a list box is being filled with a large amount of records, try limiting the amount using a statement like Where rownum < a certain number and allow for additional filtering.

ORA-00001: Unique constraint (schema_name.table_name) violated. This means a primary key violation occurred. For instance, if an Employee ID is unique, and the developer tried to insert Employee ID 99 two times, the Database will not allow it. Try changing the next value in the sequence that inserts into the primary key field for a fix.

ORA-0092: missing or invalid option.
This means there is a syntax issue possibly associated with creating a table or an object.

ORA-0093: invalid … name…
If a developer is attempting to alter a table or column name he or she should make certain to use the correct syntax for the task.

Example:

To rename the table use this syntax:
Alter table schema_name.table_name to new_table_name;

Reference:
http://docs.oracle.com/javadb/10.8.3.0/ref/rrefsqljrenametablestatement.html

Example:

To rename a column use this syntax:

Alter table schema_name.table_name rename column column_name to new_column_name;

Reference:
http://www.dba-oracle.com/t_alter_table_rename_column_syntax_example.htm

ORA-04031: unable to allocate 32 bytes of shared memory
Have the DBA extend the tablespace segment.

ORA-04062: timestamp of package has been changed
Recompile the form and possibly the package as well.

ORA-04062: Signature of package has been changed
Try to recompile the form or report or the module.

ORA-04091: Table X is mutating
This error can occur when a trigger calls another trigger that causes the initial trigger to re-fire. The ORA_UTL.WHO_CALLED_ME function can be used to determine who called this trigger and stop the mutating problem.

ORA 00936: Missing Expression
This means that part of a clause is missing. For instance, there may be a SELECT statement without a FROM or a WHERE statement.

ORA-06502: PL/SQL: Numeric or value error string
This means there is a Null variable assignment or the data type assignment is incorrect. See Decimal in the Database chapter.

ORA-06512: at "SYS.UTL_FILE", line …
If this error occus a Database directory may be missing.

ORA-01403: No data found
This could mean a SELECT INTO did not return any data. Try to verify the data exists using a COUNT before updating the variable.

ORA-01440: Column to be modified must be empty to decrease precision or scale.
If this occurs, create a new column in the table with the new required functionality, update the new field with the old values, drop or rename the first column, and rename the new field as needed.

ORA-02287: Sequence number not allowed here
Insert a value into the sequence variable.

ORA-27137: unable to extend memory segment
Have the DBA extend the tablespace segment.

ORA-29283: Invalid File Operation
If this error occurs someone may need to create a database directory.

ORA-040901: X is mutating, trigger/function may not see it.
If this occurs, it means the code is updating a table and when that happens, another piece of code is updating the table. This may lead to recursive updates leaving invalid data in the DB. Investigate using the ORA_UTIL.Who_Called_Me function for a possible fix.

REP-110: File X cannot be opened.
Make a minor change to the report (like adding a space in the PL/SQL code) and recompile.

REP-1070: An error occurred while opening or saving a document.
Make a minor change and recompile. See REP-110.

Error 905: Object Is Invalid
If the developer is unable to compile a module on the machine, he or she should try to compile it on the server or in another place.

Compilation Errors Have Occurred:
If this error occurs with no error file, attempt to export the display, ie. export DISPLAY=localhost:9.0 and make sure it is being compiled in the correct place with the correct environmental variables and syntax.

Tip:

If encountering an error with Oracle Forms or Oracle Reports a user can click CTRL + SHIFT + E to see details about the error message.

Oracle JDeveloper:

The Java based JDeveloper and Application Development Framework, as well as the Oracle Application Express IDEs have begun to take the place of Oracle Forms because they are able to produce more advanced web based Oracle applications. Read the Java chapter in this book and visit http://www.oracle.com/technetwork/developer-tools/jdev/overview/index.html for additional information. Also see http://www.oracle.com/technetwork/developer-tools/jdev/overview/index-100269.html for some JDeveloper tutorials.

Oracle Light:

This tool allows users to view and modify a subset of application data while disconnected from the Internet or the Oracle Database. A tool like this is very useful for emergency responders or service providers who require a very minimal amount of down time.

Oracle Reports:

This development tool allows a developer to create Oracle Reports and related software. These reports are used in many industries and primarily called from Oracle based Applications.

Some useful triggers and commands in Oracle Reports include:

BEFORE-PARAMETER-FORM
BEFORE-REPORT
BETWEEN-PAGES

SELECT INTO…
SRW.Message(number,'message value');

Tip:

A developer can format a Report field by right clicking it in the layout section and adding conditional formatting.

If a Report is not running or causing problems a programmer can connect to Enterprise Manager and open the Oracle Report Server queue. This queue allows administrators and developers to see what has and has not run and any associated errors. Running the report on the client is another way to troubleshoot this problem.

Tip:

It is difficult to search every Oracle Form or Report in a directory or a directory substructure. Consider using the grep32.exe application found at http://www.wingrep.com. This tool allows a user to type in a wildcard search expression, select the directories he or she want to look through, choose the file types needed, and then display the files that match his or her expression. Developers can also save Oracle Reports as an XML file and store them somewhere for directory searches.

Tip:

Ensure the tnsnames.ora and etc/hosts files are setup to resolve addresses. This is needed for server connections.

Tip:

Oracle Reports can be a memory hog. If this occurs, go to Advanced Computer Settings and click on Advanced Performance options to change the Total Paging file size to around 200000 MB.

Here are a few useful Oracle Reporting terms:

<u>Display Item</u>

This is a read only text based item.

<u>Image</u>

This is a picture or graphic displayed on the report.

<u>Label</u>

A label is used to identify a control like a text field or an image.

<u>Mickr Line</u>

The mickr line is the line on a paystub report that allows common machines to read and process information like the bank code.

Text Field

A text field is a control that displays alpha numeric data on the report, i.e. employee departments and item descriptions.

Tip:

When programming in Oracle Reports, keep multiple backups in case a rollback is needed.

Tip:

When having trouble getting a modification to take affect try putting the rdf and rep files in the "correct" locations one at a time and then retest running the report until it works.

See Oracle Forms for more details.

Oracle VM:

Oracle VM allows developers to modify and test Oracle Software in a variety of environments using a variety of tools and configurations.

Oracle Wallet:

This is a container used with Oracle DBs to provide secure authentication and authorization to System Objects. See https://docs.oracle.com/cd/B19306_01/network.102/b14266/cnctslsh.htm#g1033548 for additional information.

OWA_UTIL:

OWA_UTIL is a free Oracle library with useful tools. Here are some of the associated functions and procedures:

CalendarPrint:
This Prints a page from the Gregorian calendar if that is the calendar the developer prefers.

TablePrint:
This Prints a DB table out using an HTML format.

ToDate:
This will convert a DateType variable to a standard PL SQL Date.

Who_Called_Me:
This function will tell a programmer who called the object regardless of what it is.

Tip:

OWA_UTIL is a set of Oracle functions and procedures. The list above only includes a few of the functions available. Find out more at http://docs.oracle.com/cd/E12839_01/portal.1111/e12042/psutil.htm

Portal:

Oracle Portal is the Oracle version of a Portal. SharePoint is the Microsoft version, and WebSphere is the IBM version of a Portal.

Reference Cursors:

Developers can create Reference Cursors that will work with Oracle Forms and Reports. When creating these cursors using Oracle Forms it is necessary to specify what functions are used to insert, update, delete, and read data.

Oracle Reports only need a select function reference cursor. The nice thing about Reference Cursors is that they can select data from various places and plug it into a temporary table that is then used by the front end form or report to process and display it. If a large query is taking a long time to process somewhere this technique may work better.

Example:

The following creates hypothetical reference cursor objects needed to select and maintain data related to pants in Oracle Forms and Reports.

```
--Create the pants_ref table to retrieve clothing data for a company.
CREATE TABLE pants_ref
        (pants_id number,
      Pants_Type varchar2(100),
      Color number  --1 = blue, 2 = gray, 3 = tan, 4 = other
      );

--Assign Permissions
GRANT INSERT, SELECT, DELETE, UPDATE ON pants_ref TO
ALL;
--Create the Package
--After creating the package and body, use the Oracle Form data block
wizard to create the insert, update, and delete procedure references.
CREATE OR REPLACE PACKAGE pants_ref_package AS
TYPE pants_ref_rec IS RECORD(
pants_id pants_ref.pants_id%TYPE,
type   pants_ref.pants_type%TYPE);
TYPE pants_id_rec IS RECORD (pants_id
pants_ref.pants_id%TYPE);
TYPE pants_ref_cur IS REF CURSOR RETURN pants_ref_rec;
TYPE pants_ref_tab IS TABLE OF pants_ref_rec INDEX BY
BINARY_INTEGER;
TYPE pants_id_tab IS TABLE OF pants_id_rec INDEX BY
BINARY_INTEGER;
PROCEDURE pants_ref_query_rcur ( block_data IN OUT
pants_ref_cur, p_pants_id IN NUMBER);


PROCEDURE pants_ref_query ( block_data IN OUT pants_ref_tab,
p_pants_id IN NUMBER);
PROCEDURE pants_ref_insert (block_data IN pants_ref_tab);
PROCEDURE pants_ref_update (block_data IN pants_ref_tab);
PROCEDURE pants_ref_delete (block_data IN pants_id_tab);
PROCEDURE pants_ref_lock (block_data IN pants_id_tab);
END;


CREATE OR REPLACE PACKAGE BODY pants_ref_package AS
PROCEDURE pants_ref_query_rcur( block_data IN OUT
pants_ref_cur,
```

```
p_pants_id IN NUMBER) IS
BEGIN
OPEN block_data FOR
SELECT pants_id, pants_type, color
FROM pants_ref

WHERE pants_id = NVL(p_pants_id, pants_id)
ORDER BY pants_id;
END;


PROCEDURE pants_ref_query( block_data IN OUT pants_ref_tab,
p_pants_id IN NUMBER) IS
i NUMBER;
CURSOR pants_ref_select IS
SELECT pants_id, pants_name, pants_salary
FROM pants_ref
WHERE pants_id = NVL(p_pants_id, pants_id)
ORDER BY pants_id;
BEGIN
OPEN pants_ref_select;
i := 1;
LOOP
FETCH pants_ref_select INTO block_data(i).pants_id,
block_data(i).pants_name,
block_data(i).pants_salary;
EXIT WHEN pants_ref_select%NOTFOUND;
i := i + 1;
END LOOP;
END;


PROCEDURE pants_ref_insert(block_data IN pants_ref_tab)
IS
i NUMBER;
cnt NUMBER;
BEGIN
cnt := block_data.count;
FOR i IN 1..cnt
LOOP
```

```
INSERT INTO pants_ref(pants_id, pants_type, color)
VALUES( block_data(i).pants_id, block_data(i).pants_name,
block_data(i).pants_salary);
END LOOP;
END;

PROCEDURE pants_ref_update(block_data IN pants_ref_tab)
IS
i NUMBER;
cnt NUMBER;
BEGIN
cnt := block_data.count;
FOR i IN 1..cnt
LOOP
UPDATE pants_ref
SET pants_name = block_data(i).pants_name,
pants_salary = block_data(i).pants_salary
WHERE pants_id = block_data(i).pants_id;
END LOOP;
END;


PROCEDURE emp_ref_delete(block_data IN emp_id_tab)
IS
i NUMBER;
cnt NUMBER;
BEGIN
cnt := block_data.count;
FOR i IN 1..cnt
LOOP
DELETE FROM pants_ref WHERE pants_id = block_data(i).pants_id;
END LOOP;
END;
PROCEDURE pants_ref_lock(block_data IN pants_id_tab)
IS
i NUMBER;
cnt NUMBER;
block_rec pants_ref_rec;
BEGIN
cnt := block_data.count;
```

```
FOR i IN 1..cnt
LOOP
SELECT pants_id, pants_type, color
INTO block_rec
FROM pants_ref
WHERE pants_id = block_data(i).pants_id
FOR UPDATE OF pants_type NOWAIT;
END LOOP;
END;
END;
```

The Reference Cursor coding techniques used above were derived from the following websites:

http://docs.oracle.com/cd/B28359_01/appdev.111/b28419/d_sql.htm#CHDJDGDG
https://forums.oracle.com/forums/thread.jspa?messageID=10164017�
https://forums.oracle.com/forums/thread.jspa?threadID=273872
https://forums.oracle.com/forums/thread.jspa?messageID=981981󯯝
https://forums.oracle.com/forums/thread.jspa?threadID=620576

Searching Through Oracle Forms:

It is difficult to search every Oracle Form in a directory or a directory substructure. Use the grep32.exe application found at http://www.wingrep.com. This tool will allow a user to type in a wildcard search, select the directories to look through, choose the file types needed, and then display the files that match the search criteria.

Serialize:

Serializing is the process of taking many data parts and putting them all into a string that can be past to other programming applications.

See JSON in the chapter on Java.

Legislation

In this chapter:

1. **21 CFR 11**
2. **Section 508 Compliance**
3. **HIPPA**
4. **Protected and Disclosed Information**
5. **SOX**

21 CFR 11:

This legislation governs how electronic signatures and records must be stored in specified computer applications. See www.formulationspro.com/pages/filemaker/downloads/290.pdf for a good overview of this Legislation.

Section 508 Compliance:

Section 508 is a set of standards pulled from the Rehabilitation Act. These standards govern how Information Technology and electronic devices should be designed and developed to meet the needs of people with disabilities. Webaim provides a decent checklist for verifying whether or not an application, device, or website is compliant: http://webaim.org/standards/508/checklist. This website was used as reference for the material in this section.

Here are some points to keep in mind when designing a Section 508 compliant application, website, or tool:

> Affiliations and Partners:
>
> If a website or application is pointing to or using a third party tool or website the company should ensure that the third party tool is Section 508 compliant.

Compliance Checkers:

A compliance checker is a tool used to analyze a device, an application, or a website and report back on techniques that may need to be incorporated to make the tool compliant. Here is a list of a few compliance checkers for Section 508 compliance:

http://www.508checker.com/
http://achecker.ca/checker/index.php

Colors:

When developing a tool ask questions like if it will work for a color blind person. Designers should consider using different colors techniques when text fields or images that may be difficult to notice for certain users.

Devices:

Ensure that tools and other devices used with the application are Section 508 compliant.

Flashing:

Any flashing or loud noises that might disturb a disabled person should be eliminated.

Images:

Ensure that all images have descriptive text that will convey messages accurately using a text reader.

Grid Images And Tables:

Ensure that Grids and Tables will work with a text reader. This is especially important when a grid is being used to places small images together to make a larger image.

Script Friendliness:

Relate to the user what a piece of code is going to do before it surprises them. Example 1) If a script is going to go through a process like changing data on the screen or on the back end or displaying information differently, this should be pointed out before hand. Example 2: If a code piece is going to modify what the user has already learned or navigate them to another location the application should inform them ahead of time about the change.

Site Alternatives:

If a website is not 508 compliant, this should be conveyed to the user up front and an alternative form of communication should be provided such as a Word Document or a PDF.

Text Readers:

People with disabilities may have their text reader enabled on their computer. This will read information from the browser using the mark up language designations. These readings should thoroughly convey every idea accurately and completely. Developers need to be aware if code is going to impact the reader or cause the text reader to read unneeded characters or wording. This should be limited as much as possible.

Video:

When playing video the developer will need to ensure the media is accompanied by a Document or PDF transcript that can be read by the text reader.

Visual Aids:

Try not to use visual aids that will confuse a user. Pictures of dynamite or burning computers may not appeal to every user and may add to their confusion. ☺

Example:

Take a look at the following section for examples on how to create HTML and Java Script based websites that will or will not comply with the Section 508 guidelines.

---

1. What to do with an image map.

   The following letters.jpg image map is being used in the website example below:

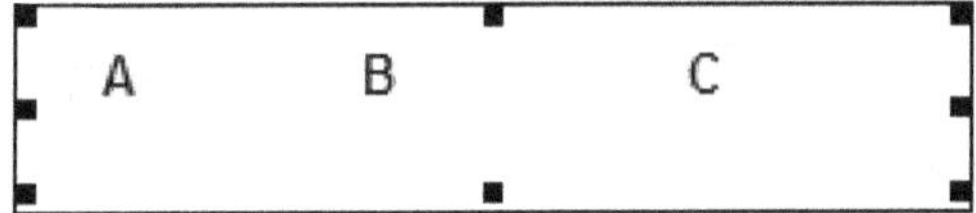

```
<!DOCTYPE html>
<HTML>
<HEAD>
<H1>Displaying a Section 508 compliant image map.</H1>
</HEAD>
<BODY>
<P><P>
<H3>The image map below contains a Letters picture map with A, B,
and C, linking to A.html, B.html, and C.html."</H3>

<img src="letters.jpg" alt="This is a Letters picture map with A, B, and
C linking to A.html, B.html, and C.html." usemap="#myImageMap">

<map name="myImageMap">
 <area coords="0,0,60,40" href="A.html" alt="A">
 <area coords="70,0,130,40" href="B.html" alt="B">
 <area coords="140,0,200,40" href="C.html" alt="C">
</map>
<P>
```

```
For the first image, the 1st X,Y position is 0, 0, and next is 60, 40.
<P>
For the second image, the X,Y position is 70, 0, and the next is 130, 40.
<P>
For the third image, the X,Y position is 140,0, and the next is 200, 40.
<P>
</BODY>
</HTML>
```

---

2. What to do with a video.

```
<HTML>
<HEAD>
</HEAD>
<BODY>

<h2>This is a video about girafes.  If you are unable to read the sub-
titles click on the transcript below:</h2>
<a href="http://www.google.com" target="_blank"> <img
src="girafes.gif" alt="This is a video about girafes."/></a>
<P>This is a video about girafes.  If you are unable to read the sub-
titles click on the transcript below."
<a target="_top" href="text_only_video.html">A text only video
transcript.</a>
</BODY>
</HTML>
```

---

3. What to do with an individual image.

```
<!DOCTYPE html>
<HTML>
<HEAD>
<H1>Displaying a Section 508 compliant image.</H1>
</HEAD>
<BODY>
<P><P>
<a href="http://www.google.com" target="_blank"> <img
src="img1.jpg" alt="This is a picture of Nebraska."/></a>
<P>
Additional website wording.
</BODY>
</HTML>
```

4. What to do with a table.

```
<!DOCTYPE html>
<HTML>
<HEAD>
<H1>Displaying a Section 508 compliant table with the th,
and title tags.</H1>
</HEAD>
```

```
<BODY>
<P><P>
<H3>The following table provides the sport name,
duration, and times for the field events:</h3>
<table id = "1" title="The following table provides the sport
name, duration, and times for the field events.">
  <tr title="row 1">
    <th scope="col" id="RaceName">Race Name</th>
    <th scope="col" id="Duration">Duration</th>
    <th scope="col" id="Time">Time</th>
  </tr>
  <tr>
    <td>Sack Race</td>
    <td>2 minutes</td>
    <td>9:00 AM</td>
  </tr>
  <tr>
    <td>Egg Race</td>
    <td>1:30 minutes</td>
    <td>9:40 AM</td>
  </tr>
</table><P>
Additional website wording.
</BODY>
</HTML>
```

---

5. How to provide a link to an alternative, text only, website.

```
<!DOCTYPE html>
<HTML>
<HEAD>
<H1>A Non Compliant Section 501 Website With A Text
Only Alternative</H1>
</HEAD>
<BODY>
<P></P>
 Create a link to a text only page if the current page is not
Section 508 Compliant.
<P></P>
     
<a target="_top" href='text_only.html'>A Text Only
Alternative Website</a>
<!...>
</BODY>
</HTML>
```

6. How to use java script to move to a different section in HTML.

```
<!DOCTYPE html>
<HTML>
<SCRIPT LANGUAGE="javascript" TYPE="text/javascript">
   function moveToBox()
      {
          alert('Inside Java Script');
      document.Disclaimer.TextName.focus();
      }
</SCRIPT>
<HEAD>
<H1> Section 501 Compliance with a Java Script move function.</H1>
</HEAD>
<BODY>
<P></P>
  Alert the user when using Java Script to do something unexpected.
     
<a target="_top" href="text_only.html">A Text Only Alternative
Website</a>
<P> Information about a specific product.
<P></P>
<form name=section508Form>
<P><H3>Click to move to the Name input box below:</H3>
<P><input alt="Click to move to the Name input box below:"
type="button" value="Click" onClick="return moveToBox();">
</form>
<P> Additional wording.
<P> Additional wording.
<P> Additional wording.
<P> Additional wording.
<P> Additional wording.
<P> Additional wording.
<P> Additional wording.
<P> Additional wording.
```

```
<P>  Additional wording.
<P>  Additional wording.
<P>  Additional wording.
<P>  Additional wording.
<P>  Additional wording.
<P>  Additional wording.
<P>  Additional wording.
<P>  Additional wording.
<P>  Additional wording.
<P>  Additional wording.
<P>  Additional wording.
<P>  Additional wording.
<P>  Additional wording.
<P>  Additional wording.
<P>  Additional wording.
<P>  Additional wording.
<P>  Additional wording.
<P>  Additional wording.
<div id="sectionName">
<P>  This is a devision section.
</div>
<P>  FDA Warning:  This product should not be used internally.
<P>  Please sign up for information about our external medication.
<form name=Disclaimer>
<P><input type="text" id="TextName" value="Please enter Name"
onkeypress = "return moveToBox();" />
<P><input type="text" id="PhoneNumber" value="Please enter Phone
#" />
</form>
</BODY>
</HTML>
```

---

7. A scrolling marquee is **"not"** compliant because it can cause some people to go into epileptic shock.

```
<!DOCTYPE html>
<HTML>
<HEAD>
<H1>Displaying a non Section 508 compliant blinking scrolling
marquee.</H1>
</HEAD>
<BODY>
<P><P>
<MARQUEE WIDTH=50%>A blinking scrolling marque like this can
cause some people to have a stroke.</MARQUEE>
<P>
Additional website wording.
</BODY>
</HTML>
```

HIPPA:

This legislation attempts to ensure that sensitive, personally identifiable information is not distributed and or displayed with data related primarily to the health care system in the US. Computer programs must ensure that the data is maintained securely according to these standards.

Protected and Disclosed Information:

There is some information that cannot be shared because it is protected by law. For instance, patient identifiers, names, and phone numbers cannot be distributed with a clinical trial because this information is protected by the Health Insurance Portability and Accountability Act.

Other information must be disclosed. For instance, the Sarbanes Oxley Legislation mandates that some accounting information must be disclosed to investors in order to allow them to make fair and accurate decisions.

www.hss.gov
www.hipaa.com
www.soxlaw.com

SOX:

This Legislation was legislated by Sarbanes and Oxley. It attempts to ensure employees are truthful and up front about paperwork related to company's sales and revenue.

Security

In this chapter:

1. Security Concepts

Security Concepts:

A+ Certification:

A person acquires an A+ certification to protect their company from various security breaches. The following is a list of items companies should consider and attempt to implement to secure users and technology related assets.

1. No password sharing.
2. Testing for strong passwords.
3. Encrypting tables with customer information.
4. Storing sensitive data in encrypted format and only displaying a portion of it in various applications.
5. Using 256 bit (or higher) password [and file] encryption.
6. Locking the server room.
7. Locking out passwords after 3 attempts.
8. Not storing sensitive customer information on paper.
9. Changing passwords within 90 days.
10. Using Captcha images where possible to prevent automated attacks.
11. No passwords or sensitive data on flashdrives.
12. Consider using an Intrusion Detection System on the firewall.
13. Following suggestions like the ones on http://www.makeuseof.com/answers/whats-the-best-way-to-block-sites-with-my-router-without-slowing-down-the-Internet/ and use the Router to setup a white or a black list of addresses that could cause problems.
14. Consider using chip and pin cards:

See https://www.ricksteves.com/travel-tips/money/chip-pin-cards.

AAA:

This stands for Authentication, Accounting, and Access. See the related definitions below.

Adware:

This simi-malicious software displays adds on a computer at random times. Some adware may have the ability to track the user's interests. Use www.adblockplus.org to block adware.

Access:

Access is the ability to see and or manipulate a piece of data or a program.

Accounting:

Accounting is the process of Auditing and checking on users as they access computer programs and objects.

Authentication:

Authentication is the process of determining that someone is who they say they are before granting them access to various assets.

Backups:

A backup is a redundant object used to ensure the object will not get lost, stolen, or corrupted.

Business Continuity Plan:

A BCP explains the storage of off site backup items, redundant sites, hardware, and software, and redundant lines of communication.

See Disaster Recovery Plan. [1]

Reference:
1. David L. Prowse, CompTIA Security + SY0-301 Authorized Cert Guide, Pearson, 2012, Page 494

Business Security Plan:

The BSP is a company wide explanation of Authentication, what software is allowed on a system, how remote access will occur, monitoring of various kinds of intrusion, and what to do if an incident occurs.

Reference:
http://www.businessnewsdaily.com/3235-business-security-plan.html

CAPTCHA:

Primarily Web based Apps may use an image request – response to determine if the user is a human or a program. This is useful with user authorization and the preventing of Denial of Service attacks.

Denial of Service:

A Denial of Service attack occurs when a computer or multiple computers attempt to access a resource so many times that the resource becomes sluggish or unable to respon altogether.

Disaster Recovery Plan:

This is very similar to a Business Continuity Plan as defined above.

Echelon:

A series of satellites used to track conversations.

Electromagnetic Microwave Pulse:

The US is building an EMP weapon that uses electric microwave pulses to disrupt an enemy computer system.

Encryption:

Encryption uses mathematics to make the values in a file cryptic for security purposes.

Exploitation

Exploitation occurs when a hacker or terrorist overcomes a security measure for malicious purposes.

Hackers:

Various hackers attempt to exploit a company's security measures with different goals. For instance, a white hat will do this to ensure that the security standards are ready for an attack. A black hat will do this with malicious intent. Other hackers will do this to sell information to the media or show off his or her computer skills to rest of the hacking community.

Kerberos:

Kerberos is a type of router used to block out security risks as they attempt to enter a localized network.

Malware:

Malware is an all encompassing term that refers to software developed with malicious intent. See Adware, Spyware, Trojan, and Virus.

Network Maintenance Plan:

A Maintenance plan documents downtimes, extended staff responsibilities, software and equipment obligations, and performance monitoring considerations for an organization.

Reference:
http://www.corpcomputerservices.com/services/maintenance

Raid:

Administrators may use different levels of RAID, or various Server disk configurations to store data multiple times or over more than one disk. RAID provides a level of data redundancy for a server.

Risk Management:

When a team performs tasks like Impact Analysis meetings they attempt to reduce the risk presented by possible future accidents and or intentional system attacks: [1]

See Business Continuity Plan for additional information

Reference:
1. David L. Prowse, CompTIA Security + SY0-301 Authorized Cert Guide, Pearson, 2012, Page 342

SAML:

This stands for Security Assertion Markup Language. It is a XML based Protocol that specifies how to secure and transmit organized data from a Destination to a Source computer and or an Application.

Security Clearance:

Various workers in the military and local law enforcement have different levels of security to infrastructures and to computer systems. For instance, someone with a high level of security may have access to everything in a building including administrative computer accounts. Someone with a low level of security clearance may just be allowed in one room to log on to one computer as a guest user.

Security Systems:

Various Operating systems have different techniques for dealing with security. Consider how administrators handle Linux permissions as opposed to handling Windows permissions.

Service Level Agreement:

A Service Level Agreement specifies reasonable connection speed, uptime for a network, network performance, and response, and on-call responsibilities for an organization providing a service. [1]

See Business Continuity Plan

Reference:

1. David L. Prowse, CompTIA Security + SY0-301 Authorized Cert Guide, Pearson, 2012, Page 528

Single Sign On:

The idea with single sign on is that the user logs in to an account using a combination of things they know, things they are, or things they have, and at this point he or she will have access to everything assigned to them in every computer system on the network. If the person needs to move from one application to another, the single sign on technology will use their initial credentials to establish new ones. A tool like a Database or an Active directory will be used to authenticate the user.

Spyware:

Spyware tracks computer use in various ways. It may utilize the webcam to watch the users actions or use a key logger to see what is being typed. It may also have the ability to track the user's interests. Readers can use a tool like the one found at www.norton.com to block spyware. [1]

Reference:

1.David L. Prowse, CompTIA Security + SY0-301 Authorized Cert Guide, Pearson, 2012, Page 21

Tape Backup:

Information Technology administrators will use tape backups as an alternative for backing up data. These tapes are light weight and look like a small hard drive. They can store a lot of data. For instance some tapes can store up to 20 gigabytes. Tape backups can be stored at an off site location so that if a catastrophe occurs and a system is wiped out, the administrator can have the tape backup delivered to the site and then he or she can restore the system. See Business Continuity Plan.

There are different methods for backing up information. Some people may backup a system every 5 or every 8 days and some people may use a group of tape backups and store the data using a complicated algorithm.

Take a look at http://en.wikipedia.org/wiki/Backup_rotation_scheme and http://enwikipedia.org/wiki/Tape_drive for additional information.

Trojans:

Ever read the story of the Greeks who fought against Troy with the Trojan horse? This is a program that uses a "friendly" application to gain access to a computer and then replicates itself for malicious purposes. Use tools like the ones found at www.viper.com and www.norton.com to detect and remove these pests. [1]

Reference:
1. David L. Prowse, CompTIA Security + SY0-301 Authorized Cert Guide, Pearson, 2012, Page 20, 30

Viruses:

A virus is a program that infiltrates a computer and recreates itself to attack other computers. It can use Microsoft VBA to accomplish this tasks. Examples include the I Love You and the Melissa viruses. Use the Microsoft security settings and tools found at www.viper.com and www.norton.com to detect and remove pests like viruses and Trojans, and to detect security breaches like a hacker connecting into their system. [1]

Reference:
1. David L. Prowse, CompTIA Security + SY0-301 Authorized Cert Guide, Pearson, 2012, Page 18, 19

Users should not map drives from their computer to computers on another network. They should also be careful not to click on popups. If an unexpect popup occurs it is advisable to unplug the Network cable altogether. Some viruses based on the CryptoWall virus can hold encrypted files ransom until someone pays to have the files decrypted. [1]

Reference:
1. Joseph J. Krueger, ATS | Director, IT Services, 7-Nov-2014

Glossary

.NET: A Microsoft IDE featuring many programming languages.
21 CFR 11: This set of rules explains how to file important information in a computer.

A+ Certification: A popular security certification.
AAA: Access Authentication and Authorization
Abstract Class: A cookie cutter template Java class.
Access: A Microsoft Database used with small projects.
Accounting: A concept relating to the auditing, loging, and reporting of security related activities in a company.
ACL: Acces Control List
Action Request System: See Remedy and Test Track.
Active Directory: A Microsoft tool used to govern computer permissions and activities over an Enterprise or Company wide network.
Activity Diagram: A flow diagram used to represent the actions taken within an Application or program piece.
ADO Connections: ActiveX Data Objects used to make various kinds of connections to various kind of data containers. This tool is used primarily in Microsoft .NET.
Adobe PDF: A document tool used heavily on the Internet.
Adware: Quasi-malware used to popup messages and advertisements through an Application or a Web Browser.
AGILE: This is a cyclical programming method that goes through stages of customer interaction, design, development, prototyping, and customer verification.
AJAX: Asynchronous Javascript and XML
Aperture: A tool used to diagram objects (like Network objects) and locations within a company or enterprise.

Apple: The computer company that is recognized for designing the popular Mac computer, the iphone, and the ipad.
Applet: A Java program that runs on its own within a web browser.
Application: A group of code pieces, forms, reports, and other objects used to provide a service to a user community.
Application Layer: This is a group of forms, reports, or other objects used to allow users to update and look at data within a company. See Open Systems Interconnection (OSI) Model.
Artificial Intelligence: This is the idea that computers can be trained to reason, learn, and contribute like an intelligent life form.
ASP: Active Server Pages
AspectJ: A language that deals with Cross Cutting Concerns. A cross cutting convern occurs with a Java event. An example would be a login that needs logged.
aspx: An ASP file extension.
Assembly Language: A low-level language that works closely with machine level commands.
Authentication: This occurs when a user proves that he or she is the person they claim to be. This can be done using techniques like providing a password or a biometric feature.
avi: An Audio Video Interleave file extension.

Bcc and CC: Blind copy and carbon copy.
Bigram: A two number or character combination.
Binary: A numeric positioning of numbers that features a base of two. A one in the first position is one. A one in the

second position is two. A one in the third position is four, etc.

Binary Code: Code based on binary values.
Boiler Plate Object: A reusable text object.
Boolean: A yes or no value.
Borland: This company features software development tools such as the Star Team and Caliber.
Branching: When Application code is modified in different ways, ie. for different versions, the saved versions will need to be “branched” in a change control system.
Browser: This is a tool used to display websites or Internet based Applications.
Btree: A binary assortment of information or objects.
Bubble Sort: A sorting technique that compares values one at a time putting each value in a required sort order.
Business Continuity Plan: A document used to explain how a company will continue to function after a specified or non specified problem occurs.
Business Security Plan: A document used to explain how security measures should be inacted within an organization.

CAPTCHA:
Primarily Web based Apps may use an image request – response to determine if the user is a human or a program. This is useful with user authorization and the preventing Denial of Service attacks.
Captivate: A tool used to create presentations.
Case: A statement used to switch between alternate events and output depending on a predefined condition.
Cat: A command used to output a file to the monitor.
Certificates: A SSL object used to authenticate a user by incorporating user specific encrypted information in files and messages passed between a client and a server.

Checksum: A value used to determine if a message, file, or string has been changed as it travels across the Internet or a Network.
Class: A file used to define and refine object properties and methods within an Application.
ClickYes Pro 2010: A tool used to auto click an input button using a coded command.
Client: A general user will use a client computer to compute or connect to a larger computer system.
CLOB: Character Large Object.
Cloud Technology: Services and tools provided via an assortment of unknown service provider machines and products.
Coalesce: A command that returns the first non null value for each record within a delimited set of values.
Code Review: The concept of having someone else review code before it is tested or implemented in Production.
Combo Box: A selection box displaying a set of values and returning a set of representational values in an Application. Users are able to select from the list but not type into it.
Command Prompt: A prompt used in a few Operating Systems to accept commands and return output.
Comments: Remarks made within code to explain what it does, who did it, when it was done, and other information.
Commit: To save changes especially when using SQL.
Component: This is a term used with modern languages such as Java explaining how separate code modules work together to provide various Application functionality.
Connection String: A string used to connect to a Database or Operating System or other object.
Console Application: A stand alone application usually used to perform a specific task like creating a report.

Constraint: A Database rule that ensures various objects conform to predefinied business requirements.
Container: An object that groups similar items together.
Content Management System: A system, like Google Docs, that allows users in various groups and roles to access various documents as allowed by the community.
Continue: A command that tells the program to move on to the next iteration within a code segment.
Contingency Plan: This is the plan a company uses if things go wrong.
Control: This usually refers to an item in an IDE.
Contract: When an organization officially decides to use a company to deliver a service.
Cookies: Web Browser Files used to track user responses and properties on a client.
Copy and Paste: The idea of copying a value from one place or Application to another.
Cowboy Programming: Programming by the seat of the pants without checks and balances.
CRC: See Checksum.
CRON: CRON is used in the UNIX world. The Greek word Cronos means time. A cron job runs at a specified time to perform a specified request.
CRUD: This DB term stands for Create, Update, and Delete.
Crystal Reports: An easy to use reporting tool that pulls data from a variety of sources with various formatting and grouping capabilites.
csh: A Corn Shell script file extension.
css: A Cascading Style Sheet file extension.
csv: A comma separated values file extension.
Cursors: Cursors are used with Database tables to cycle through data and perform specific tasks.

Cute FTP: A cuter version of the File Transfer Protocol.

Database: A group of tables and other objects used to store information about a company, object, or other organization(s).
Data Set: A set of table or lookup data.
Data Types: Integers, Characters, Booleans, and Date are all examples of types used to define Application objects.
Data Warehouse: A data repository used for analysis and reporting.
Database: A tool used to collect and maintain data for a company or organization.
Database Trigger: An event that runs code when a specified Database event occurs like a login.
Date: A specified day and month in a specified year. Examples include 1/1/2014 and 1-Jan-2015. Dates may include the time as well.
DB Link: A link from one DB to another.
DBA: Database Administrator.
DCL: DIGITAL Command Language.
Debugging: This is the process of determining why a piece of code is not working properly.
Decimal: This is a value that occurs after the integer portion of a number. In other words, this is found after the decimal.
Declare: A statement used to mark the starting point of a code section in a PL/SQL or T-SQL block. The statement is used to declare variables before code is executed.
Decode: A command used to return a default value or different output values with different input values.
Decryption: Using a mathematical algorithm to return encrypted values back to a human readable format.

Denial of Service: A hacking attack that occurs when one or more computers attempt to access a server in order to make it perform less efficiently.
Design Document: A document used to define details about how a program should be built.
Dijkstra: A mathematician who created an algorithm for determining the shortest path between coordinate sets.
Disaster Recovery Plan: A plan used to explain how a company will recover if an emergency or disaster occurs.
Discrete Structures: This deals with math objects that can only take on a single or a discrete value.
Distributed System Solution: Using various technology to provide a System Solution.
Distribution List: An email list for distributing messages.
DML: Data Manipulation Language
DNS: Domain Name System

eBlvd: This is an Internet Application that performs helpdesk ticket support.
Echelon: Satelites used to track conversations for security purposes.
Eclipse: A development environment used to create Java Applications.
Email: An Electronic Mail program.
Encryption: Transforming a string, value, or an entire file into an unreadable format that can be reverted using a mathematical process.
Enigma Machine: A World War II machine used to encode messages sent by the Germans.
Enterprise Business Suite: A suite of business applications produced by Oracle for an enterprise or another large organization.

Entity Data Model: A model created in .NET that allows code to interact with it and then select and modify the source data.
Etc Host: This is a file that tracks hosts used with Oracle Internet Applications.
Excel: A Microsoft Spreadsheet Application.
Exit: To move out of an Application releasing variable values and other computer resources.
Exploitation: To take advantage of a security system for malicious purposes.

Faraday Cage: This is a room inside of a building that is designed to prevent any kind of technology communication from going in or out.
Fail Over Database: If a database or a database server stops working data and connections can be "ported" or moved to a fail over database so that work on the data can continue.
File Comparison: A tool used to see where files differ.
Filezilla: An open-source FTP product.
Fine Grained Access: A Database concept that tracks many events occurring within the Database and can be used audit the events for security purposes.
Finite State Representation
Flash: This is a tool used by programmers to make java based web applications look nicer.
Foreign Key Constraint: This constraint ensures that a value exists in another table before it can be used in the table the user is working with.
Fortran: An older programming language with block coding conventions.

Function: A code piece that performs a specific task like adding two numbers. Functions do not usually return values, but they can in some languages.
Fuzzy Logic: A logic that does not deal with absolutes.

Garbage Collection: The concept of releasing variables and resources when they are no longer used in a code piece or an Application.
Get: To pull data and store it in a structure so it can be viewed, set, and released by the underlying Application.
Glassdoor: A Website used to gain inside information about a company of interest.
Global Assembly Cache: A .NET container that houses configurations and settings for an Application.
Global Temporary Table: A session related table that stores data for temporary purposes like displaying report information.
Global Variable: A variable that can be used in various places associated with an Application.
Google Docs: See Content Management System.
Google Glass: A pair of glasses users can wear to see computer output and collaborate with other users.
Google Maps: This program allows users to hewn in on and see specific locations on the map at an unspecified point in time.
Google Plus: This Website features many social services such as document collaboration and personalized web pages.
Google Translate: A Website used to translate phrases from one language to another.
GoTo: A statement used to move from one place to another in a program. The use of this command is discouraged.

Greedy Algorithm: An alrgorithm that looks for the simplest way to achieve each local goal until the global goal is reached.
grep: A Unix based tool or command used to locate an expression in a file or files located in a specified location on a computer.
grep32: A Windows tool or command used to locate an expression in a file or files located in a specified location on a computer.

Hacker: Different kinds of computer people who usually want to cause computer related issues for a company or organization.
Hardware: The actual physical objects used in a computer or system of computers.
Hashing: Assigning fixed values to a set of values in order to organize them for mathematical purposes.
Heap: A specific type of tree structure.
Hexadecimal: A numeric positioning of numbers that features a base of sixteen. See binary.
HIPPA: The Health Insurance Portability and Accountability Act.
Host: A Server hosting programs and services for clients.
HTML: Hypertext Markup Language.

IBM: International Business Machines.
IBM Cube Technology: An IBM programming language that works with Excel VBA to query table values using three or more parameters.
IDE: An Integrated Development Environment.
Image: A picture used in a document or Application.
Index: An ordered numeric or string set of values used to locate records in a table or file.

Infopath: A Microsoft tool used to create forms.
Inheritence: In OOP this occurs when one object aquires traits from another by incorporating its class properties and capabilities .
Inline View: When a Select statement is found inside the FROM clause of a query.
Instant Message (IM): A tool used to allow users to communicate text messages across the Internet or over a Network.
Instantiation: When an object first takes on the characteristics and default variable values and methods of a class.
Instr: A function used to determine where a value occurs within a string.
Intellisense: A type ahead feature of many modern tools.
Interface: A code piece that is called to interact with properties and methods in a class.
Internet: An interconnected group of networks.
Intrusion Detection System: This program will let people know if someone or something is trying to get in and cause problems on a computer network.
Intrusion Prevention System: This program will attempt to stop someone or something from trying to get in and cause problems on a computer network.
IP Layer: These are the Internet Protocol "addresses" used to pass information from one computer to another on the network or over the Internet.
ISP: Internet Service Provider.
Iterate: To move to the next item in a set of objects.

Java: A language used by programmers to build applications, websites, and other tools used by computer people.

JavaBean: A class with many objects that can be passed between different programs in a Java Application.
Java Script: A Java based language used primarily with HTML web pages to manipulate data and other page items.
Java Server Faces: A component based Java specification.
Jdeveloper: An Oracle tool used to develop Java code and Applications.
Join: A command used to "join" one or more Database tables together.
Jquery: A JavaScript library used to query Database data.
js: The JavaScript file extension.
JSF: Java Server Faces
JSON: JavaScript Object Notation
jsp: The Java Server Pages file extention.
Junit: A tool used to create scripted tests against Java based code.

Kerberos: A ticket based protocol used to authenticate users on a Network.
Keyboard Shortcuts: A series of a few keys that can be used together to perform tasks like copying and pasting.
Knapsack Problem: A mathematical prolem that utilizes the Greedy Algorithm to assign items to knapsacks.

License: An agreement made physically or digitally that allows a user to use a software program giving them rights to use the software in a predefined way.
LINQ: Language Integrated Query
LINUX: An OS whose origin and name originated from Linus Torvalds who worked to enhance a version of Unix named Minix.
List: A table like object used in Microsoft SharePoint.

List Box: A group of values used in a Form or Report. Users are able to select from the list but not type into it.
Lock: A "lock" occurs when an object, like a table or record, is secured so it cannot be modified by a user while another user is making changes to it.
Logic: The use of mathematics and science to determine the truth about a given problem.
Long: A large numeric datatype
Lower: A function used to format a string as lower case.
LPAD: Removes spaces located on the left of a string.

Malware: Any malicious software such as adware, spyware, or a virus that is developed with the intent to exploit or obtain information from the user.
Mapquest:: A website used to provide maps and suggest the best directions from one physical location to another.
Materialized View: This is a view that offers data persistence. See persistence below.
Membership Services: A .NET feature that uses tables and procedures to implement user and group security in an Application.
Microsoft: A computer company that provides many software related tools to businesses around the world.
Microsoft Project: A tool used to manage project details.
Minus: A SQL command used to remove a set of data from another set of data.
Mobile Device: A device that can connect to useful applications on a server, or over a network or Internet.
Mod: A command used to return the remainder of a dividend value.
Movie Maker: A Microsoft tool used to produce movies. This tool comes free on many Windows Operatin Systems.
Mp4: A file used to display images and sounds.

MySQL: A popular open-source Database.

Netbeans: An IDE used to produce code using Java, C++, HTML and other popular languages.
Network: A series of Servers and Clients working together. A Network is a technology used to relate computers together so they can communicate more efficiently.
Network Maintenance Plan: A company used to explain how a Network topology should be maintained.
Network Topology: An arrangement of computers and cables and other equipment like routers to ensure hardware and data redundancy and efficient communication

Object Oriented Database: A DB based on Object Oriented principles.
Object Oriented Programming: A programming methodology that revolves around object characteristics and actions.
ODBC: Open Database Connectivity
Office 365: A Microsoft cloud service allowing companies and users to utilize a combination of products and support packages.
olb: An Object Library file extension.
Operating System: A programming platform that other programs run on.
Operator Precedence: This is used to determine what mathematical operations occur first in a program.
Oracle: A computer company that provides many software related tools to businesses around the world.
Oracle Application Development Framework: A Development Framework based on PL/SQL and Java programming.

Oracle Application Express: An Oracle development environment that creates DB products for the Web.
Oracle Application Testing Software: This tool can be used to automatically test software using predefined techniques.
Oracle Database: A Database system provided by Oracle.
Oracle Database Connectivity (ODBC): Some Oracle applications use ODBC drivers to permit users to access table data in a database.
Oracle Developer Suite: This suite includes the Oracle Forms and Oracle Reports IDEs.
Oracle Forms: An Oracle IDE used to create Forms.
Oracle Jdeveloper: An Oracle IDE used to create Java Applications.
Oracle Light: This product allows users to run DB Applications on a disconnected client machine and modify the DB at a later point.
Oracle Reports: An Oracle IDE used to create Oracle Reports.
Oracle VM: Oracle Virtual Machine is used to test software in a variety of environments with different accompanying objects to ensure a product will work effectively,
Oracle Wallet: Oracle Wallet is a Java based Application that stores authentication information in a secure DB.
Open Systems Interconnection (OSI) Model: This model describes how hardware and software is used at different layers to present data to users.
OTR: Off the Record works with Pidgin to provider a more secure Instant Message experience.
Over: An SQL statement allowing a developer to run a function over a specified filter and return that value in every record.

OWA_UTIL: An Oracle utility library used to provide a variety of functionality.

Package: An Oracle object consisting of a specification and a body file with variables and modules. These files are used together to achieve different results.
Paint: A Microsoft product used to create illustrations and images.
Paintshop Pro: A program used to create illustrations and pictures.
Partition By: An SQL statement allowing a developer to run a function over a specified filter group and return that value for every related record group.
PcAnywhere: This program allows a user to control another computer on the Network or over the Internet.
Performance: The overall effectiveness of an Operatins System, a Program, or another object.
Perl: A tool that downloads on the server and allows a programmer to work closely with values in the OS or in a Database residing there.
Persistence: This refers to the concept of being able to see data and object characteristic at a specific point in time.
Physical Layer: These are the wires, nuts, bolts, monitors, keyboard, and other hardware devices used in computer companies today.
Pidgin: An Instant Messaging tool.
Pivot: A command that allows a user to look at or modify table data by pivoting the rows and columns.
Pointer: An object that references a place in memory where an array or structure resides.
Port: A virtual server object that a program must connect to in order to utilize a service like Telnet or SMTP.

Power Point: A Microsoft tool used to create Presentations.
Primary Key Constraint: A key constraint that ensures a record can be uniquely identified via a unique field value.
PrimeFaces: These are JSF components that add additional functionality for the framework.
Procedure: A piece of code that can accept parameters and usuall returns a value.
Properties: Values like color and length used to describe an item in an Application.
Proprietary: Not intended for general use.
Push And Pop: A technique used for storing and retrieving information from a data stack.
PVCS: Polytron Version Control System.

Quality Testing and Customer Review: Techniques used to ensure Software works as expected before being implemented in Production.
Quick Time: A Program used to play movie media on a computer.

Radio Group: A record selection used in PL/SQL based Applications.
RAID: Redundant Arry of Inexpensive Disks.
RDBMS: Relational Database Management System.
rdf: An Oracle Reports file extension.
Reconcile: This refers to the process of ensuring two sets of data match.
Record Set: A Microsoft collection of records displayed in an Applicatin.
Recursion: When a program calls itself multiple times to achieve a result this is known as recursion.

Reference Cursor: This refers to a DB program that uses a Cursor to select and maintain data for a front end Application like an Oracle Form.
Refresh: To refresh a data set with the latest values.
Regular Expression: An expression used to look for a pattern in a string or a document.
Remedy: A ticketing system used to track detailed project parts assigned to various team members.
Remote Desktop: A tool used to remotely control another computer on the Network or over the Internet.
Replace: A function used to replace one value with another.
Report Builder: An Oracle tool used to build reports.
Required Field: A required table field must be supplied when a record is created.
REST: Representation State Transfer.
Rich Faces: These are JSF components that add additional functionality for the framework.
Risk Management: This is the mitigation of risk by discussing it and planning for it ahead of time.
Risk Mitigation Plan: This plan helps companies to be as functional and profitable as possible when an emergency occurs.
Role: A group of permissions assigned to a user set.
Rollback: This command will undo a set of SQL commands unless a commit is issued explicitly or implicitly.
Root Server: A key Internet Server that stores addresses and traffic patters essential to the Internet infrastructure.
RPAD: Removes spaces located on the right of a string.

SAML: Security Assertion Markup Language
Savepoint: A statement that tells the SQL where to rollback to if a Rollback is issued.
Schema: A container usually associated with a user that contains objects within a Database.
scp: The secure copy command can be used to copy data from one place to another in a secure fashion.
Screen Cover: A monitor cover used to protect it.
Screen Saver: A screen saver shuts the monitor off or puts it in a hyernating state after a while to save resources.
Search Engine: A browser tool used to search Websites for content.
Section 501 Compliance: Legislation that governs how programs should interact with people who have disabilities.
Security Clearance: A security ranking that someone has for accessing various levels of sensitive information.
SendMail: An Oracle package used to send mail.
Sequence: A DB object used to increment a number that is usually used as unique identifier in a table.
Serialize: To put multiple data pieces into a String format so it can be passed around in the Application.
Server: A more robust computer used to provide additional software related tools.
Service Level Agreement: A two party agreement that defines the responsiblities of the users and party supplying the computer Services.
Session: A group of variables and other objects related to a user when he or she logs into an OS or a DB. The session uniquely relates a user to the System and should be removed when the user logs out.
Set: To store data changes in the underlying location so the Application can get the data and use it later.

Setup File: A file used to setup an application on a computer.
SFTP: Simple File Transfer Protocol.
sh: This is a shell script file extension.
SharePoint: The Microsoft Protocol IDE.
Silverlight: This is a Microsoft tool used by programmers to make mobile and web applications look nicer.
Single Sign On: This is the concept of being authenticated once once and then having access to every tool and service permited for a given user.
Smart Tags: Some browsers and Document tools have search items call Smart Tags that allow a user to see every occurance of an item when clicking on it.
SMS: Short Message Service
SMTP: Simple Mail Transfer Protocol
SnagIt: This tool allows users to snag a piece of the screen, manipulate and save it, and find object coordinates within the picture.
SOAP: Simple Object Acces Protocol
Socket: The combination of a username, password, and Server Port is refered to as a Socket.
Software: Programs that run on the hardware of a computer.
Sound Recorder: A Microsoft OS Application used to record sounds.
Source: The computer that is providing a Service or an object like a data file.
Sarbanes and Oxley: These two congressmen wrote some laws to ensure people tell the truth about the money and the products their company makes.
Sprint: Sometime Software Project timelines are refered to as sprints.

Spyware: Malware used to spy on a computer user in a variety of ways.
SQL: Standard Query Language
SQL Server: A Database system provided by Microsoft.
SQLLDR: SQL Loader
SSL: Secure Socket Layer
Stateless Session Bean: A JavaBean that does not contain client specific information.
Struct: A data type that is complex and groups a list of variables together in an organized way. A struct can be used to represent a table or a similar object. Structs are found in the C language.
Subnet Mask: When networking computer together, engineers can use different Subnet Masks classes (generally A-C) to control what TCPIP addresses will be used with the Domain Controller and other Servers and Clients on the Network.
Substring: This function takes a string and a starting position and an ending position and returns the values between these two locations.
Subversion: This is a free tool used to control and store both old and new Software Versions. The Version Control piece integrates with Tortoise SVN on the Client side to provide additional functionality. Subversion.apache.org/
Swift: This programming language uses a variation of the C# language in order to build robust apps that function with the iOS and iOS X platforms
Sync: This command can be run for an Oracle DB to synchronize DB pieces or an entire DB Schema with another DB such as a testing DB.
Synonym: A synonym creates an alias for a DB object. A synonym can be used so that users can select and

manipulate an object in another DB schema as if it exists in the current DB schema.
SysDate: This is the Current Date from the OS on the Server hosting the DB.
System Table: This is an underlying Database table that is used to store general information about users, permissions, tables, and other objects in the System.
System Variable: These can be found in a UNIX operating system. They are used to set environmental variable information specific to the user or system.

Table: A group of rows and columns used to maintain the characteristics of objects in a company. For instance, a department or an employee may be stored in a table.
Tar: A command used commonly on UNIX machines to shrink files. Untar is used restore the file to its original content.
TCL: Tool Command Language
Terminal Server: This is a lightweight computer that can be hooked up to a Network and used for purposes like remote troubleshooting of Network devices.
Test Track: A ticketing system used to track detailed project parts assigned to various team members.
Text Item: An alpha numeric item used in forms and reports and documens.
Themes and Branding: These are used to mark a piece of software so that other people know who created it or who paid for it.
Thread: Coding threads are used to run separate processes in an Application.
Timezone: A world time system based on the Greenwitch mean time.
To_Char: A function used to convert a value to a string.

To_Date: A function used to convert a value to a Date.
Toad: A tool used to work with a SQL Server or Oracle Database. It offers many capabilites from table selection to the setup of users and roles.
Topology Map: This is a map used to display where the network perimeter is at and how it is laid out within an organization. Some network types include meshes and trees.
Tortoise SVN: This client software integrates with subversion to provide client side version control functionality.
Trigger: Triggers fire and perform a series of commands when events occur for a Database object.
Trigram: A three number or character combination.
Trojan Horse: A computer virus that disguises itself as friendly software to gain access to a computer or a network.
Try Catch, and Finally: A series of statements used in .NET to catch exceptions, throw them to their calling objects, and finalize processing.
T-SQL: Transact-SQL is used to perform SQL commands with Microsoft products such as .NET.
Turing Machine: This is a hypothetical machine that was conceived by Alan Turing in the 1930s.

Unifield Modeling Language (UML): With this language developers are allowed to draw out complicated system designs and, in many circumstances, use the language to generate the code.
Union: This command will take two selected datasets and return every unique record. See Union All.
Union All: This command will take two selected datasets and return each record from the selection. See Union.

Unit Test Script: A set of tests used by a programmer to ensure an application works.
Use Case Scenarios: Various requirement scenarios an application should provide.
UNIX: An Operating System that uses typed responses with a command prompt.
Uptime: This tool is used to determine the availability or uptime of a remote computer on the network.
User: A person using a client or server or other computer device.
Using: A statement used in languages like C and Visual basic to let the system know an object will be used and released for a program related purpose.

Varidesk: A desk that folds or rises as the user desires.
VBA: Visual Basic for Applcations.
VBS: Visual Basic Scripts.
VINN Diagram: A diagram used to show Unions, intersections, outliers, and other relationships between groups.
Virus: A malicious program that infects and spreads.
Visual Basic: A visual programming language. VBA is based off of Visual Basic.
VPN: A Virtual Private Network.

WAR: A file used to deploy Java code.
Waterfall Programming: A method of programming that moves from one cycle to a new cycle as water flows downstream through a waterfall system.
Web Part: Coding pieces used to display data and perform other tasks in Microsoft SharePoint.

Web Services: These services are used across applications. The services provid useful information like accurate dates and times or organized relational data.
Wildcards: Filter expressions used to locate specific information in a file or Database i.e. %ing would be used to find words ending with ing.
Winzip: A tool used to mathematically shrink a file to a smaller size and the extract the file contents later.
Wireshark: A tool used to view data in various forms as it moves across the Network.
Wmv: A file used to display movies and play sounds.
Word: A Microsoft tool used to create documents.
WWW: The World Wide Web
XML: The Extended Markup Language.
XML Spy: A tool used to open, create, and update XML files.

Yesware: Quasi-malware software used to determine how many times an email successfully reaches another party.

Zone: A technique used to group computers on a Network.

Index

Biography

Phillip Ray Garriss has been a computer programmer for over 15 years. He has written articles for the ODTUG journal and has a paper published by UNCW which he completed for his Masters Degree in Computer Science and Information Systems. He has several computer certifications and has taught classes on Oracle, Microsoft, and CISCO Fundamentals at Miller-Motte technical college. Phillip works as an Application Developer II at Applied Technology Solutions (http://www.ats.coop/) in Castle Hayne, NC. This company develops accounting software for electric coops around the United States and has taught him a wealth of knowledge. His hobbies include Hebraic and Latin Biblical studies which he does with his family. He and his family have written several books including "Bill And Martha" and "Fire Red and Adriana Start A Computer Company" and "Perpetual Motion 7". The family also enjoys biking and swimming.

www.ingramcontent.com/pod-product-compliance
Lightning Source LLC
Chambersburg PA
CBHW080402060326
40689CB00019B/4107

* 9 7 8 1 0 7 7 5 2 5 9 8 6 *